Teach Yourself®

Get started in Modern Hebrew

Shula Gilboa

Advisory editor
Gila Mielke

T0385233

First published in Great Britain in 2013 by Hodder & Stoughton. An Hachette UK company.

This edition published 2013

Copyright © Shula Gilboa

British Library Cataloguing in Publication Data: a catalogue record for this title is available from the British Library.

Library of Congress Catalog Card Number: on file.

ISBN 9781444175110

10 9 8

The publisher has used its best endeavours to ensure that any website addresses referred to in this book are correct and active at the time of going to press. However, the publisher and the author have no responsibility for the websites and can make no guarantee that a site will remain live or that the content will remain relevant, decent or appropriate.

The publisher has made every effort to mark as such all words which it believes to be trademarks. The publisher should also like to make it clear that the presence of a word in the book, whether marked or unmarked, in no way affects its legal status as a trademark.

Every reasonable effort has been made by the publisher to trace the copyright holders of material in this book. Any errors or omissions should be notified in writing to the publisher, who will endeavour to rectify the situation for any reprints and future editions.

Cover photograph: © Yuriy Chertok/Fotolia.

Typeset by Integra Software Services Pvt. Ltd., Pondicherry, India

Printed and bound in Great Britain by Clays Ltd, Elcograf S.p.A.

Hodder & Stoughton policy is to use papers that are natural, renewable and recyclable products and made from wood grown in sustainable forests. The logging and manufacturing processes are expected to conform to the environmental regulations of the country of origin.

Hodder & Stoughton Ltd

338 Euston Road

London NW1 3BH

www.hodder.co.uk

Contents

About the author

Dr Shula Gilboa has many years of experience in teaching Hebrew and running teachers' seminars in Israel, Australia, New Zealand and England.

How the book works

Hebrew learners need to familiarize themselves with the alphabet: consonants and vowels. The alphabet will be introduced later in the book, accompanied with exercises, to practise and memorize the new alphabet.

Get Started in Hebrew is composed of ten units, each dedicated to one topic, including: greetings and introductions, family life and staying in a hotel. Each unit is aimed at covering the four linguistic skills: listening, speaking, reading and writing, and throughout each unit there are exercises to help you practise these skills. Following Unit 3 and Unit 6, you will have the chance to practise the material you have already learned in a review section. At the end of Unit 10, you will find an extended review section to help you learn everyday Hebrew, as it is spoken on the streets of Israel.

In addition to the alphabet section, ten units and three reviews, you can find in this book:
▶ Learn to learn – a useful guide to help you in learning a new language.
▶ A list of useful expressions.
▶ Pronunciation guide.
▶ Answer key for all exercises.
▶ The vocabulary acquired in this book.

Learn to learn

The Discovery method

There are lots of approaches to language learning, some practical, some quite unconventional. Perhaps you know of a few, or even have some techniques of your own. In this book we have incorporated the **Discovery Method** of learning, a sort of DIY approach to language learning. What this means is that you will be encouraged throughout the course to engage your mind and figure out the language for yourself, through identifying patterns, understanding grammar concepts, noticing words that are similar to English, and more. This method promotes language awareness, a critical skill in acquiring a new language. As a result of your own efforts, you will be able to better retain what you have learned, use it with confidence, and, even better, apply those same skills to continuing to learn the language (or, indeed, another one) on your own after you've finished this book.

Everyone can succeed in learning a language – the key is to know how to learn it. Learning is more than just reading or memorizing grammar and vocabulary. It's about being an active learner, learning in real contexts, and, most importantly, using what you've learned in different situations. Simply put, if you figure something out for yourself, you're more likely to understand it. And when you use what you've learned, you're more likely to remember it.

And because many of the essential but (let's admit it!) dull details, such as grammar rules, are taught through the **Discovery method**, you'll have more fun while learning. Soon, the language will start to make sense and you'll be relying on your own intuition to construct original sentences independently, not just listening and repeating.

Enjoy yourself!

Tips for success

1 MAKE A HABIT OUT OF LEARNING

Study a little every day, between 20 and 30 minutes if possible, rather than two to three hours in one session. Give yourself short-term goals, e.g. work out how long you'll spend on a particular unit and work within the time limit. This will help you to create a study habit, much in the same way you would a sport or music. You will need to concentrate, so try to create an environment conducive to learning which is calm and quiet and free from distractions. As you study, do not worry about your mistakes or the things you can't remember or understand. Languages settle differently in our brains, but gradually the language will become clearer as your brain starts to make new connections. Just give yourself enough time and you will succeed.

2 EXPAND YOUR LANGUAGE CONTACT

As part of your study habit, try to take other opportunities to expose yourself to the language. As well as using this book you could try listening to radio and television or reading articles and blogs. Perhaps you could find information in Hebrew about a personal passion or hobby or even a news story that interests you. In time you'll find that your vocabulary and language recognition deepen and you'll become used to a range of writing and speaking styles.

3 VOCABULARY

Group new words under **common roots** such as family members or food; **situations** in which they occur, such as, for asking directions: crossroads, traffic lights, left, right, subway station; and **functions** such as greetings, parting, thanks, apologizing. Say the words out loud as you read them.

Write the words over and over again. Remember that if you want to keep lists on your smartphone or tablet you can usually switch the keyboard language to make sure you are able to include all accents and special characters.

▶ Listen to the audio several times.
▶ Cover up the English side of the vocabulary list and see if you remember the meaning of the word.
▶ Associate the words with similar sounding words in English, e.g. קפה (**kafe**) and סוכר (**sukar**) with *coffee* and *sugar*.
▶ Create flash cards, drawings and mind maps.

- ▶ Write words for objects around your house and stick them to these objects.
- ▶ Pay attention to patterns in words.
- ▶ Experiment with words. Use the words that you learn in new contexts and find out if they are correct.

4 GRAMMAR

- ▶ To organize the study of grammar write your own grammar glossary and add new information and examples as you go along.
- ▶ Experiment with grammar rules. Sit back and reflect on the rules you learn. See how they compare with your own language or other languages you may already speak. Try to find out some rules on your own and be ready to spot the exceptions. By doing this you'll remember the rules better and get a feel for the language.
- ▶ Try to find examples of grammar in conversations or other articles.
- ▶ Keep a 'pattern bank' that organizes examples that can be listed under the structures you've learned.
- ▶ Use old vocabulary to practise new grammar structures.
- ▶ When you learn a new verb form, write the conjugation of several different verbs you know that follow the same form.

5 PRONUNCIATION

- ▶ When organizing the study of pronunciation keep a section of your notebook for pronunciation rules and practise those that trouble you.
- ▶ Repeat all of the conversations, line by line. Listen to yourself and try to mimic what you hear.
- ▶ Record yourself and compare yourself to a native speaker.
- ▶ Make a list of words that give you trouble and practise them.
- ▶ Study individual sounds, then full words.
- ▶ Don't forget, it's not just about pronouncing letters and words correctly, but using the right intonation. So, when practising words and sentences, mimic the rising and falling intonation of native speakers.

6 LISTENING AND READING

The conversations in this book include questions to help guide you in your understanding. But you can go further by following some of these tips.

- ▶ Imagine the situation. When listening to or reading the conversations, try to imagine where the scene is taking place and who the main characters are. Let your experience of the world help you guess the meaning of the conversation, e.g. if a conversation takes place in a snack bar you can predict the kind of vocabulary that is being used.

▶ Concentrate on the main part. When watching a foreign film you usually get the meaning of the whole story from a few individual shots. Understanding a foreign conversation or article is similar. Concentrate on the main parts to get the message and don't worry about individual words.

▶ Guess the key words; if you cannot, ask or look them up.

7 SPEAKING

Rehearse in Hebrew. As all language teachers will assure you, the successful learners are those students who overcome their inhibitions and get into situations where they must speak, write and listen to the foreign language. Here are some useful tips to help you practise speaking Hebrew:

▶ Hold a conversation with yourself, using the conversations of the units as models and the structures you have learnt previously.

▶ After you have conducted a transaction with a salesperson, clerk or waiter in your own language, pretend that you have to do it in Hebrew, e.g. buying groceries, ordering food, drinks and so on.

▶ Look at objects around you and try to name them in Hebrew.

▶ Look at people around you and try to describe them in detail.

▶ Try to answer all of the questions in the book out loud.

▶ Say the dialogues out loud then try to replace sentences with ones that are true for you.

▶ Try to role play different situations in the book.

8 LEARN FROM YOUR ERRORS

Don't let errors interfere with getting your message across. Making errors is part of any normal learning process, but some people get so worried that they won't say anything unless they are sure it is correct. This leads to a vicious circle as the less they say, the less practice they get and the more mistakes they make.

Note the seriousness of errors. Many errors are not serious as they do not affect the meaning. So concentrate on getting your message across and learn from your mistakes.

9 LEARN TO COPE WITH UNCERTAINTY

▶ Don't over-use your dictionary. Don't be tempted to look up every word you don't know. Underline new ones and read or listen to the passage several times, concentrating on trying to get the gist of the passage. If after the third time there are still words which prevent you from getting the general meaning of the passage, look them up in the dictionary.

▶ Don't panic if you don't understand. Just keep going and try to guess what is being said and keep following the conversation or, if you cannot, isolate the expression or words you haven't understood and have them explained to you.

▶ Keep talking. The best way to improve your fluency in the foreign language is to talk every time you have the opportunity to do so: keep the conversations flowing and don't worry about the mistakes. If you get stuck for a particular word, don't let the conversation stop; paraphrase or replace the unknown word with one you do know, even if you have to simplify what you want to say. As a last resort use the word from your own language and pronounce it in an Israeli accent.

AND FINALLY

1. Most Hebrew words have a three-letter root, so learning these roots can be helpful in recognizing and memorizing words.

2. One of the difficulties in learning Hebrew is the lack of vowels. In this book, in order to familiarize the learner with the vocabulary, Hebrew words are accompanied with transliteration (the Hebrew words in English letters).

Useful expressions

סליחה, אני לא מבין	Slicha, ani lo mevin.	*Sorry, I don't understand.*
?אתה יכול לחזור על זה ?את יכולה לחזור על זה	Ata (m) yachol lachazor al ze? At (f) yechola lachazor al ze?	*Can you repeat it?*
?אתה יכול לדבר לאט יותר ?את יכולה לאט יותר	Ata (m) yachol ledaber yoter le'at? At (f) yechola ledaber yoter le'at?	*Can you speak more slowly?*
?סליחה, מה השעה	Slicha, ma ha'sha'a?	*Excuse me, What is the time?*
?...סליחה, איפה ה תחנת משטרה בית חולים בנקומט תחנת אוטובוס תחנת רכבת רחוב רבין	Slicha, eifo ha...? tachanat mishtara beit cholim bankomat (bank + automat) tachanat otobus tachanat rakevet Rechov Rabin	*Excuse me, where is the...?* *police station* *hospital* *cashpoint* *bus station* *train station* *Rabin street*
?...אפשר לקבל כוס מים כדור נגד כאב ראש	Efshar lekabel...? kos mayim kadur neged ke'ev rosh.	*May I have...?* *a glass of water* *a pill against headache*
?...אפשר לקבל כרטיס ל קונצרט, תאטרון, קולנוע, אוטובוס, רכבת	Efshar lekabel kartis la...? concert, teatron, kolnoa, otobus, rakevet	*May I have a ticket to the...?* *(concert, theatre, cinema, bus, train)*
שלום נעים מאוד ?מי אתה תודה תודה רבה לא, תודה	Shalom. Na'im me'od. Mi ata? Toda. Toda raba. Lo, toda.	*Hello.* *Pleased to meet you.* *Who are you?* *Thank you.* *Thank you very much.* *No, thank you.*
?אפשר לקבל חשבון ?כמה זה עולה ?זה כולל טיפ	Efshar lekabel cheshbon? Kama ze ole? Ze kolel tip?	*May I have the bill?* *How much does it cost?* *Does it include the tip?*
?מתי זה מתחיל ?מתי האוטובוס יצא ?מתי הרכבת יוצאת ?מתי המטוס יצא	Matay ze matchil? Matay ha'otobus (m) yotze? Matay harakevet (f)yotzet? Matay hamatos (m)yotze?	*When does it start?* *When does the bus leave?* *When does the train leave?* *When does the plane leave?*

Pronunciation

In every language some of the pronunciation and writing rules are tricky. This is even more so when it comes to languages with non-Latin alphabets. When learning a new language, gradual acquaintance with rules during the process of learning, is recommended. Nevertheless, here are a few pointers on pronouncing and writing in Hebrew, which you will come across in this book.

VOWELS

As you will learn from the forthcoming Alphabet section, Hebrew vowels are either consonantal or appear as dots and dashes above, below and in the middle of the consonant. Most texts you will come across (with the exception of the Bible, prayer-book and poetry) are without the dots and dashes. This makes it hard for beginners, and this is why, in this book, every newly introduced word is also written in Latin letters.

A short reminder

▶ The consonantal vowel ו sounds like *o* (*boy*), or like *u* (*book*). For example: כדור (**kadur**, *ball*); חור (**chor**, *hole*). The letter ו is also a consonant, and then it sounds like *v*, for example: וילון (**vilon**, *curtain*).

▶ The consonantal vowel י sounds like *e* (*bee*). For example: תמיד (**tamid**, *always*). The letter י is also a consonant, when it sounds like: ירוק (**yarok**, *green*)

DIFFERENT LETTERS PRONOUNCED SIMILARLY

The following letters are pronounced similarly: ש, שׁ/ ע, א / ט, ת / כ, ח. Why is that?

ח and ע are throaty letters, which are pronounced differently from כ and א which are palatal letters. For several reasons, most Hebrew speaking people in Israel (even radio broadcasters) don't differentiate between palatal and throaty letters, but the differentiation in writing has not changed. This is why ח sounds like כ, and א sounds like ע. For instance: the words אור (*light*) and עור (*skin*) sound alike: **or**. In the word חכם (*clever*) both letters sound alike: **chacham**.

There is no distinction between ת and ט in Modern Hebrew. English speakers can find a writing clue in international words. **th** = ת; **t** = ט. For instance:

theatre	תיאטרון
tango	טנגו
theodor	תאודור

Another pair of letters is שׁ (**sh**) & שׂ (**s**). Without dots, they look alike and in most cases are pronounced sh.

LETTERS PRONOUNCED DIFFERENTLY, ACCORDING TO THEIR PLACEMENT

Three letters פ, כ, ב sound differently when at the beginning of a word or a syllable, and when placed elsewhere. For example:

ב	בית	**bayit**	*house*	רחוב	**rechov**	*street*
כ	כלב	**kelev**	*dog*	סבתא	**savta**	*grandmother*
פ	פרח	**perach**	*flower*	חוף	**chof**	*beach*

The letter ח (**ch**) when at the end of a word following the consonantal vowel sounds like ach.

רוח	**ruach**	*wind*	מדיח	**madiach**	*dishwasher*
תפוח	**tapuach**	*apple*	שיח	**siach**	*nush*
כוח	**koach**	*strength*	אבטיח	**avatiach**	*watermelon*

LETTERS PRONOUNCED DIFFERENTLY WHEN WRITTEN WITH AN APOSTROPHE

▶ The letter צ (**tz** – there is no equivalent in English) with an apostrophe 'צ sounds like *ch* in *Charles*.

▶ The letter ג (like *g* in *good*) with an apostrophe 'ג sounds like the second *g* in *gorge*.

The Hebrew alphabet

Shalom שלום. You are about to get started with your first lesson in Modern Hebrew עברית (**Ivrit**).

As you may be aware, you are about to embark on a journey of discovery by learning a language which is ancient in its origin, but is also one of the newest languages around today.

As an introduction, you will learn the symbols of the Hebrew alphabet אלף-בית (**aleph-bet**). This will allow you to identify Hebrew consonants and vowels and will give you a better grasp of the script. This is only an elementary step, and further practice with the written script will be covered in the more advanced *Teach Yourself Complete Modern Hebrew* course.

Historical snapshot

The Hebrew alphabet is comprised of 22 letters, and was developed alongside other Middle Eastern languages during the late second and first millennia BC.

The invention of the alphabet was a huge development from the pictorial script. It replaced a great numbers of signs and symbols with a small number of letters, creating a far easier code of expression.

Around 2,000 BC, the ancient script used in the land of Israel and Syria was the Proto-Canaanite script. This was sometimes written from right to left, and sometimes from left to right. Hebrew script as we know it evolved from the Phoenician script, around the 11th century BC. The Phoenicians finalized the shape of the letters, reduced the number of letters to 22 and introduced the final direction of the text —from right to left.

Following the exile of the Jewish people from the land of *Israel* ישראל (**Yisrael**) and the destruction of the Jewish temple, in 70 AD, *Hebrew* עברית (**Ivrit**) was no longer in spoken use, but survived as the language of Biblical and religious texts. It is a very different story today and there are now more than 7 million speakers of עברית in the world.

In the late 19th century the lexicographer, Eliezer Ben-Yehuda, was part of a movement which set about reviving Hebrew. It is now the official language of Israel and is in spoken use throughout the world.

Hebrew עברית (**Ivrit**) is a Semitic language. The group of Semitic languages has its origins in ancient Canaan and includes Aramaic and Arabic. Modern Hebrew, which you are about to start learning, is based on the Biblical, oral-law and Middle Ages Hebrew. This means that in mastering the modern language, you will be able to understand some of the ancient dialect as well.

As in the English language, the names of the Hebrew letters are related to their vocal expressions. Most of the letters have parallels in English. However, unlike English, the Hebrew אלף-בית is a consonantal one. This means that there are no separate letters for vowels. Instead, vowels are marked as lines and dots. Two letters, **vav** and **yod** can function as consonantal vowels.

Alphabet in script

In the first part of the section, you will be introduced to the first ten letters of the alphabet and the three consonantal vowels. The handwritten script is included for your reference, but in this book you will only need to familiarize yourself with the printed form.

The first ten consonants

Name of Hebrew letter	Hebrew print	Hebrew script	English Equivalent
aleph	א	**k**	a
bet	בּ	**ⅅ**	b
vet	ב	**ⅅ**	v
gimel	ג	**ₑ**	g
dalet	ד	**ₑ**	d
hey	ה	**ⅅ**	h
vav	ו	**/**	v
zayin	ז	**ₑ**	z
chet	ח	**ₙ**	ch*
tet	ט	**6**	t
yod	י	**,**	y

LANGUAGE POINTS TO REMEMBER

▶ The letter ב with a dot in its middle is pronounced b, without the dot it is v.
▶ The letter (ג,'ג) sounds like the g in go. When the ('ג) is written with an apostrophe, it is pronounced like the g in the name George.
▶ There is no vocal equivalent in English to the letter **chet** ח. It sounds like the end of the word loch (Scotland). In this book it will be written **ch**.
▶ The letter א can be either silent or with vowels, as you will see in the following pronunciation exercise.

PRONUNCIATION

Pronounce the letters, then say the words in English. The bold letter sounds like the Hebrew letter.

א	k	**a**pple	ו	l	**v**ery
ב ב	ב ב	**b**oy **v**oice	ז	ז	**z**ebra
ג	ג	**g**ood **G**eorge	ח	ח	lo**ch**
ד	ד	**d**esk	ט	ט	**t**ry
ה	ה	**h**ello	י	י	**y**ellow

PRACTICE 1

Match the Hebrew letters to their English equivalent.

י   ט   ח   ז   ו   ה   ד   ג   ב   א

___   ___   ___   ___   ___   ___   ___   ___   ___   ___

CONSONANTAL VOWELS

The first three vowels to be learned are the consonantal vowels.
▶ The letter ו (**vav**) with a dot above it sounds like the vowel o, as in boy.
▶ The letter ו (**vav**) with a dot in its middle sounds like the vowel u, like loose.
▶ The letter י (**yod**) with a dot under the letter before it sounds like e, as in geese.

PRACTICE 2

1 Read out loud and practise the sounds of the following consonants and vowels together.

בִּי בֵי גוֹ הוּ הוֹ זִי דִי חִי אוֹ וּו וֹו טְי

דוֹ גְי זְי הוּ טְי וּו אִי

2 Read these Hebrew words.

טוב	**tov**	*good*
אוֹ	**o**	*or*
הוּא	**hoo**	*he*
הִיא	**hee**	*she*

3 00.01 **Listen and identify the consonantal vowels.**

דִי הוּגוּ זוּ הִי בוֹ בוֹ אִי גוֹ טוּּחִי

טְי גְי בוּ בוֹ הוּ

4 Read these syllables out loud.

הוּ / הוּ בוֹ / בוֹ בוּ/בוּ / גְי / גִי / גְי דוֹ / דוּ

חוּ /חוֹ / אִי / אִי טוֹב / טוֹב

Introducing the next 12 letters and dotted vowels

In this second section you will be introduced to the last 12 letters of the alphabet אלֶף-בֵית. You will also be introduced to the vowels which appear as dots and dashes above, below and in the middle of the consonant. Five Hebrew letters are formed differently when they appear as the last letter of a word.

ALPHABET IN PRINT AND SCRIPT

English equivalent	Hebrew print	Hebrew script	Final letter print	Final letter script	Name of Hebrew letter
k	כ	כ	ך	ק	kaf
ch	כ	כ			chaf
l	ל	ל			lamed
m	מ	N	ם	מ	mem
n	נ	J	ן	/	nun
s	ס	ο			samech
a	ע	✗			ayin
p	פ	∂	ף	℘	peh
f	פ	∂			feh

ts	צ	*3*	ץ	*9*	tsady
k	ק	*P*			kof
r	ר	*ꞇ*			resh
sh	שׁ	*e*			shin
s	שׂ	*ė*			sin
t	ת	*♪*			tav

 Look at the letters above. What do you notice about the following letters: kaf / chaf; peh / feh; shin / sin? (Tip: Think about the relationship between the letters ב / .בּ)

Did you notice that the sound of the letters is determined by the dots?

B = בּ V = ב K = כּ CH = כ F = פ P = פּ SH = שׁ S = שׂ

LANGUAGE POINTS TO REMEMBER

▶ Note the difference between the **kaf** and **chaf**. The pronounced like the *ch* (as in loch) and the **kaf** like letter *k*.

▶ The addition of the dot in the פ transfers the sound from *f* to *p*.

▶ Note the difference between the שׁ and the שׂ. If the dot is placed on the top right side it sounds like *sh*. When placed on the left side, it sounds like *s*.

 Practice 3

Match the Hebrew letter to the English equivalent.

ת	שׂ	שׁ	ר	ק	צ	'צ	פ	בּ	ע	ס	נ	מ	ל	כ	בּ
s	n	m	l	ch	k	ts	t	s	sh	r	k	ch	f	p	a

The vowels

The vowels **kamatz** and **patach** sound the same and are pronounced as *a* in the word class, and appear as dots under the letters. In the following example, the **patach** is shown under the **aleph** and **kamatz** under the **bet**.

father   aba   אַבָּא

The vowels **segol** and **tseire** sound like *e* in *never* and appear beneath the letters. The **tseire** is shown under the **samech** and the **segol** under the **feh**.

book   sefer   סֵפֶר

The vowel **shva** is silent: *chips* צִ׳יפְּס. The letter ה at the end of the word is silent. This is shown under the **lamed** below.

girl **yalda** יַלְדָה

PRACTICE 4

Read the following consonants and vowels:

צַ צָ שֵׁ שֶׁ בְ בָ סַ תְ נ גֶ לְ

READING WITHOUT VOWELS

You will find out that Hebrew texts and signs are usually written without dots (vowels), making it hard to decode. In this book you will find the transliteration for each word in Hebrew. This will help you with your first steps in Hebrew.

VOCABULARY

Did you know that many Hebrew words are already familiar to you? Read through and memorize these examples.

Category	Hebrew	Pronunciation	English
Places	אפריקה	Afrika	Africa
	אמריקה	Amerika	America
	אסיה	Asia	Asia
	אוסטרליה	Ostralia	Australia
	אילת	Eilat	Eilat (Israeli town)
	אירופה	Eiropa	Europe
	ישראל	Yisrael	Israel
	יפו	Yafo	Jaffa
	ירושלים	Yerushalayim	Jerusalem
	מצדה	Metzada	Massada
	נצרת	Natzrat	Nazareth
	תל-אביב	Tel-aviv	Tel-aviv
	פארק	park	park
Food	בננה	banana	banana
	בירה	bira	beer
	צ׳יפס	chips	chips (fries)
	שוקולד	shokolad	chocolate
	קפה	kafe	coffee
	פיצה	pizza	pizza
	ספגטי	spaghetti	spaghetti
	סטייק	steak	steak
	תה	te	tea

Transportation	הליקופטר	**helicopter**	*helicopter*
	ג'יפ	**jeep**	*jeep*
	טקסי	**taxi**	*taxi*
	טרקטור	**tractor**	*tractor*
Animals	ג'ירף	**giraffe**	*giraffe*
	דולפין	**dolphin**	*dolphin*
	זברה	**zebra**	*zebra*
Art and culture	מוסיקה	**musica**	*music*
	קונצרט	**contzert**	*concert*
	תאטרון	**teatron**	*theatre*
	גיטרה	**gitara**	*guitar*
Communication	אינטרנט	**Internet**	*Internet*
	רדיו	**radio**	*radio*
	טלפון	**telephone**	*telephone*
	טלביזיה	**televizia**	*television*
Money	דולר	**dollar**	*dollar*
	פאונד	**pound**	*pound*
	שקל	**shekel**	*shekel*
	יורו	**euro**	*euro*

Greetings and introductions

In this unit you will learn how to:
▶ *say hello and goodbye.*
▶ *give your name.*
▶ *give common greetings.*
▶ *say where you are from.*

CEFR *(A1): Can introduce yourself and others and ask and answer questions about personal details. Can indicate if you are following or not following conversations.*

 !ברוך הבא *(Baruch ha'bah)* Welcome!

Israel is both rich in culture and history. From the museums, art galleries, restaurants and nightlife of תל-אביב (**Tel-Aviv**), to the ancient ruins of ירושלים (**Jerusalem**), to the קיבוצים **kibbutzim**, you will find Israel an exciting country with a rich history to explore.

ישראל (**Yisrael**) is a young ארץ (**eretz**) country and only gained independence in 1948. Over the years, it has become a developed country and an OECD member and is the only country in the world with a Jewish majority population. It is the smallest country in the Middle East, with over 7 million מיליון citizens, of which 20 per cent are Arabs, most of whom follow Islam. The official languages are עברית (**Ivrit**) Hebrew and ערבית (**Aravit**) Arabic.

> Look at the Hebrew words above. Do you know the English name of the capital city of ארץ ישראל? Can you guess the English names of the biblical cities of נצרת (**Nazeret**) and בית לחם (**Bet Lechem**)?

Vocabulary builder

GREETINGS AND INTRODUCTIONS

01.01 **Listen and repeat the following words.**

בוקר	boker	*morning*
ערב	erev	*evening*
לילה	laila	*night*
טוב	tov	*good*
שלום	shalom	*hello*
בוקר טוב	boker tov	*good morning*
ערב טוב	erev tov	*good evening*
לילה טוב	laila tov	*good night*
להתראות	lehitraot	*see you / until next time*

Now see if you can complete the missing English by reading the Hebrew.

a	Good _____	ערב טוב
b	Good _____	לילה טוב
c	Good _____	בוקר טוב
d	_____	שלום
e	_____	להתראות

> **TIP**
> Good evening is actually said 'evening good' or ערב טוב (**erev tov**).
> The word Hello שלום (**Shalom**) in Hebrew also means *peace*.

NEW EXPRESSIONS

01.02 **Listen and repeat these new words and expressions.**

מי אתה? (m)	Mi ata? (m)	*Who are you?*
מי את? (f)	Mi at? (f)	
אני...	ani...	*I am...*
נעים מאוד	na'eem meod	*pleased to meet you*
טוב תודה, ואתה?	Tov toda, veata? (m)	*Good, thank you, and you?*
טוב תודה, ואת?	Tov toda veat? (f)	
אני לא מבין	ani lo mevin (m)	*I don't understand*
אני לא מבינה	ani lo mevina (f)	
אתה מדבר אנגלית?	Ata medaber Anglit? (m)	*Do you speak English?*
את מדברת אנגלית?	At medaberet Anglit? (f)	
כן	ken	*yes*
לא	lo	*no*

אני דן, מי את?
ani dan, mi at?

אני שרה, מי אתה?
ani sara, mi atah?

Conversation and comprehension

01.03 *Ron Green* רון גרין has just arrived in Israel and is meeting Mr Cohen מר כוהן for the first time. Listen to the conversation.

1 Can you identify what time of day it is that they meet?

Mr Cohen	Boker tov.	בוקר טוב.
Ron	Boker tov.	בוקר טוב.
Mr Cohen	Ani dan, Mi ata?	אני דן, מי אתה?
Ron	Ani Ron, naim meod.	אני רון, נעים מאוד.
Dan	Ata rotze kafe?	אתה רוצה קפה?
Ron	Ani lo mevin. Ata mevin Anglit?	אני לא מבין. אתה מבין אנגלית?
Dan	Ken, ani mevin. Eifo ata gar?	כן, אני מבין. איפה אתה גר?
Ron	Ani me'anglia.	אני מאנגליה.
Dan	Ata rotze kafe?	אתה רוצה קפה?
Ron	Lo, toda.	לא, תודה.
Dan	Shalom, lehitraot.	שלום, להתראות.
Ron	Lehitraot!	להתראות!

2 Listen to the conversation again and find the expressions that mean the following:

a Do you want some coffee?

b See you! Goodbye.

c Who are you?

d Do you understand English?

e Pleased to meet you.

f Good morning.

3 Now listen to the conversation again and say it out loud in Hebrew.

4 Match these questions and answers.

a	?מי אתה (Mi ata?)	**1**	אני דן. (Ani Dan.)
b	?אתה מדבר עברית (Ata medaber Ivrit?)	**2**	לא, תודה. אני לא רוצה קפה. (Lo, toda, ani lo rotze kafe.)
c	?אתה רוצה קפה (Ata rotze kafe?)	**3**	כן, אני מבין אנגלית. (Ken, ani mevin Anglit.)
d	?מה שלומך (Ma shlomcha?)	**4**	לא, אני לא מדבר עברית. (Lo, ani lo medaber Ivrit.)
e	?אתה מבין אנגלית (Ata mevin Anglit?)	**5**	טוב, תודה. (Tov, toda.)
f	?איפה אתה גר (Eifo ata gar?)	**6**	אני גר באנגליה. (Ani gar be'Anglia.)

In Hebrew there is no word for *do. Do you speak English?* is simply *You speak English?* ?אתה מדבר אנגלית **Ata medaber Anglit?**.

 Language discovery

PRONOUNS

Verbs, nouns and adjectives have masculine and feminine forms. Here are the main forms of the pronouns.

I	ani	אני	אני	*we*	anachnu	אנחנו	אנחנו
you (m)	ata	אתה	אתה	*you* (m. pl)	atem	אתם	אתם
you (f)	at	את	את	*you* (f. pl)	aten	אתן	אתן
he (m)	hoo	הוא	הוא	*they* (m)	hem	הם	הם
she (f)	hee	היא	היא	*they* (f)	hen	הן	הן

SINGULAR AND PLURAL FORMS OF THE VERB

Each verb has a root that changes in form depending on whether the pronoun attached to it is masculine or feminine, singular or plural. Most verbs have three letter roots. The root of *speak* is ה.ב.ר, *understand* is ב.י.ן, and *want* is ה.צ.ה.

MASCULINE AND FEMININE

In Hebrew there is a distinction between male and female, singular, and plural forms of words: אתה. Look at how the masculine verbs *want* רוצה and speak מדבר agree with the gender of the pronoun you אתה. Now look at the table. What are the characteristics of the male and female verbs in singular and plural forms?

	speak		**understand**		**want**	
m/s	מדבר	medaber	מבין	mev**in**	רוצה	rotz**e**
f/s	מדברת	medaber**et**	מבינה	mevin**a**	רוצה	rotz**a**
m/p	מדברים	medabr**im**	מבינים	mevin**im**	רוצים	rotz**im**
f/p	מדברות	medabr**ot**	מבינות	mevin**ot**	רוצות	rotz**ot**

Can you tell what the characteristics are? Masculine singular forms end with the root and no additions. Feminine singular forms end in the suffix ת. Masculine plural forms end in the suffix ים. Feminine plural forms end in the suffix ות.

Practice

Notice and remember some similarities and differences between English and Hebrew: *(Do) you?* = **Ata?** (אתה?); *or* = **o** (או); *tea* = **te** (תה)

1 Use the words you know to say the following in Hebrew.
   a Do you speak English?
   b I speak Hebrew.
   c Do you understand?
   d Do you want tea or coffee?

2 Say the following expressions in Hebrew.
   a Hello
   b Good night
   c See you
   d Good evening
   e Good morning

3 01.04 **Listen and repeat, then write down whether these words are singular or plural forms? Can you also identify whether they are masculine (m) or feminine (f)?**
   a אתה (ata) _____
   b הן (hen) _____
   c הם (hem) _____
   d אנחנו (anachnu) _____
   e היא (hee) _____

4 Fill in the missing word. You can also say it out loud to practise what you have learned.

a Good morning, who are you?   ?בוקר _____, מי אתה

b I am Dan, who are you?   ?אני דן, _____ את

c I am Ruth.   _____ רות

d How are you? Good, thank you.   .מה שלומך? _____ תודה

e Do you speak Hebrew?   ?אתה _____ עברית

f No, I don't speak Hebrew   לא, _____ לא מדבר עברית

g Do you understand Hebrew?   ?את מבינה _____ עברית

h Yes, I understand Hebrew (as feminine, singular).   כן, אני _____ עברית

5 01.05 Listen and repeat, and then try to answer these questions in Hebrew. Make sure that you listen out for the masculine and feminine forms and respond accordingly.

a ?מי את

b ?או: מי אתה

c ?אתה רוצה קפה

d ?את רוצה קפה

e ?מה שלומך

f ?מה שלומך

Verbs, question words and connectives

Read these regular verbs carefully, paying attention to masculine, feminine, singular and plural endings.

VERBS

	to live (dwell)		to go (travel)	
(m/s)	גר	**gar**	נוסע	**nose'a**
(f/s)	גרה	**gara**	נוסעת	**nosa'at**
(m/p)	גרים	**garim**	נוסעים	**nos'im**
(f/p)	גרות	**garot**	נוסעות	**nos'ot**

 PRACTICE

1 Read the following and write down whether each word is masculine or feminine, singular or plural?

מדבר   medaber _____   רוצה   rotze _____   מבין   mevin _____

מדברת   medaberet _____   רוצה   rotza _____   מבינה   mevina _____

מדברים	medabrim _____	רוצים	rotzim _____	מבינים	mevinim _____	
מדברות	medabrot _____	רוצות	rotzot _____	מבינות	mevinot _____	
נוסע	nose'a _____	גר	gar _____			
נוסעת	nosa'at _____	גרה	gara _____			
נוסעים	nos'im _____	גרים	garim _____			
נוסעות	nos'ot _____	גרות	garot _____			

CONNECTIVES

The one-letter connectives below are attached to the word that follows.

To London – לונדון = ל + לונדון = ללונדון (lelondon)

From London – לונדון = מ + לונדון = מלונדון (milondon)

In Israel – ישראל = ב + ישראל = בישראל (beyisrael)

Dan and Ruth – ו רות = דן ו + רות = דן ורות (dan verut)

 01.06 Listen and repeat these question words and connectives.

when?	מתי?	**matay?**	from	...מ	**me...**
where?	איפה	**eifo?**	to	...ל	**le...**
where to?	לאן?	**le'an?**	in, at	...ב	**be**
why?	למה?	**lama?**	but	אבל	**aval**
and	ו	**ve**	too	גם	**gam**

> **TIP**
> Remember that feminine singular verbs usually end with ת ,ה and the feminine plural words usually end with ת.

 PRACTICE

2 Choose the right word.

a רות (גר / גרה) _____ בישראל

b דן נוסע _____ תל-אביב _____ ירושלים (מ / ל)

c ירושלים _____ תל-אביב _____ ישראל (ב / ו)

d רות לא מדברת אנגלית (אבל / גם) _____ מבינה.

e דן מבין אנגלית (וגם / אבל) _____ מדבר.

3 Select the correct word from the choice.

גר / חה / הוא / רוצה / נוסעת

a   דן _____ באנגליה

b   רות _____ מלונדון

c   אני _____ קפה

d   הוא לא רוצה _____

e   אני, אתה ו _____

Go further

In Hebrew the names of the months from the Gregorian calendar sound similar to those in English.

Month	חודש	Chodesh
January	ינואר	Yanuar
February	פברואר	Februar
March	מרץ	Mertz
April	אפריל	April
May	מאי	May
June	יוני	Yuni
July	יולי	Yuli
August	אוגוסט	Ogust
September	ספטמבר	September
October	אוקטובר	October
November	נובמבר	November
December	דצמבר	December

Test yourself

1 Can you match the English with the Hebrew?

a	Hello.	1	טוב, תודה
b	How are you?	2	שלום
c	Good, thank you.	3	?מה שלומך
d	Until next time.	4	להתראות

2 Complete the sentences with the correct verb from the list below.

לא מבינה גר נוסעת רוצה מדבר

a Marat Green ‏מרת גרין _____ לאנגליה.

b Mar Brown ‏מר בראון _____ עברית

c Rut ‏רות _____ קפה.

d Dan ‏דן _____ בישראל

e Marat Cohen ‏מרת כוהן _____ אנגלית

3 Match these English words to their Hebrew equivalents.

and   to   in   from

a	ל	c	ב
b	מ	d	ו

4 Complete the sentences, both questions and answers, with the correct pronoun.

a _____ רוצה קפה? כן, תודה, _____ רוצה קפה.   Do you (m/s)

b _____ רוצה קפה? לא, תודה, _____ לא רוצה קפה.   Do you (f/s)

c _____ מבינים עברית? _____ לא מבינים עברית   Do you (m/p)

d _____ מדברות אנגלית? כן, אנחנו מדברות אנגלית.   Do you (f/p)

e _____ רוצה תה? כן, היא רוצה תה.   Does she (f/s)

10

SELF CHECK

I CAN. . .

○	. . . say hello and goodbye.
○	. . . give my name.
○	. . . express common greetings and say where I am from.
○	. . . identify the difference between masculine and feminine forms.

Family life

In this unit you will learn how to:
- *ask someone how they are, and reply.*
- *describe yourself and your family members.*
- *describe a person's appearance.*
- *engage with people about work and studies.*

CEFR: *(A1) Can recognize familiar words and basic phrases about yourself, your family and concrete surroundings. Can talk about members of your family.*

A family: mother אמא, father אבא, girl בת and boy בן, grandmother סבתא and grandfather סבא.

The Israeli family

Leo Tolstoy's book *Anna Karenina* begins: 'Happy families are all alike; every unhappy family is unhappy in its own way.' Israel has many different family histories ביוגרפיות, most of them with origins from around the globe. The Israeli family משפחה includes refugees from Arab countries and holocaust survivors, as well as Jewish and Arab natives.

The tapestry of Israeli family sociology סוציולוגיה continues to develop. At the close of the twentieth century, for example, Israel absorbed Jewish refugees from the former Soviet Union and Ethiopia. Even with this varied mix of cultures, each family unit still shares some common identifiable traits which we will explore together in this unit.

Look at the picture תמונה (tmuna) above and identify the following family members:

a אבא **aba**
b אימא **ima**
c בן **ben**
d סבתא **savta**

12

Vocabulary builder

 ## DESCRIBING FAMILY MEMBERS

 02.01 Listen and repeat these words that relate to family members and family life.

אבא	אבא	aba	*father*
אימא	אימא	ima	*mother*
בן / בן	בן / בן	ben	*boy (or son)*
בת / בת	בת / בת	bat	*girl (or daughter)*
אח	אח	ach	*brother*
אחות	אחות	achot	*sister*
סבא	סבא	saba	*grandfather*
סבתא	סבתא	savta	*grandmother*
משפחה	משפחה	mishpacha (f)	*family*
זה	זה	ze (m)	*this is*
זו (זאת)	זו (זאת)	zo (or zot) (f)	*this is*
ה (התמונה)	ה (התמונה)	ha (hatmuna)	*the (the picture)*
תמונה	תמונה	tmuna (f)	*picture (photo)*

In the first lesson you learned feminine singular verbs regularly end with ה, or ת. You also learned that feminine plural verbs regularly end with ות, and masculine plural usually end with ים. This same rule applies to nouns.

NEW EXPRESSIONS

To introduce a person or thing, using *this is*, you use the masculine זה **ze**, or feminine זו **zo**.

זה אבא	ze aba	*this is father*
זו אימא	zo ima	*this is mother*
זו תמונה של משפחה	zo tmuna shel mishpacha	*this is a picture of a family*
זו התמונה של המשפחה	zo hatmuna shel hamishpacha	*this is the picture of the family*

Conversation and comprehension 1

2.02 *Dan is showing Sarah a photo of his family. Listen to their conversation while you follow the text.*

1 About whom is Dan talking?

Dan	ze saba.	.זה סבא
Sarah	mi zo?	?מי זו
Dan	zo ima.	.זו אימא
Sarah	bat kama hee?	?בת כמה היא
Dan	hee bat 40.	.היא בת 40
Sarah	saba vesavta beyisrael?	?סבא וסבתא בישראל
Dan	ken hem beyisrael.	.כן, הם בישראל

2 How old is Dan's mother?

3 Where do Dan's grandparents live?

 Practice

 1 Make sure you know what the following words mean. Look them up in a dictionary if you need to: ben, aba, tmuna, saba.

2 Match the following Hebrew names for family members with their translations:

a	אבא	aba	1	daughters
b	סבתא	savta	2	father
c	בנות	banot	3	grandmothers
d	סבתות	savtot	4	grandmother

3 Remember that אנחנו anachnu means *we* and הם hem means *they*. What do שלכם shelachem and שלנו shelanu mean?

POSSESSIVE PRONOUNS

You have already learned the personal pronouns: *I, you, he, she, we, you* (plural) and *they*. Now you are going to learn the possessive pronouns: *mine, yours* and *our*.

14

של **shel** means *of*, or *to belong* and אני **ani** means I. When using a possessive pronoun, these words are contracted, for example, *mine*: + של אני = שלי **shel** + **ani** = **sheli**.

Some of the suffixes of the personal pronouns **ani** and the possessive pronouns **sheli** sound similar.

SINGULAR

שלי	שלי	**sheli**	*my / mine*
שלך	שלך	**shelcha** (m)	*your / yours*
שלך	שלך	**shelach** (f)	*your / yours*
שלו	שלו	**shelo**	*his*
שלה	שלה	**shela**	*her / hers*

PLURAL

שלנו	שלנו	**shelanu**	*our / ours*
שלכם	שלכם	**shelachem** (m)	*your / yours*
שלכן	שלכן	**shelachen** (f)	*your / yours*
שלהם	שלהם	**shelahem** (m)	*their / theirs*
שלהן	שלהן	**shelahen** (f)	*their / theirs*

PRACTICE

1 Try and match the singular personal pronouns with their possessive.

a	אני	ani		1	שלו	shelo
b	אתה	ata (m)		2	שלך	shelach (f)
c	את	at (f)		3	שלך	shelcha (m)
d	הוא	hoo (m)		4	שלי	sheli
e	היא	hee (f)		5	שלה	shela

2 **Select the correct possessive pronoun from the options provided below. Take note of the gender specified.**
  a your (m): שלכם or שלכן
  b our: שלהם or שלנו
  c their (f): שלכן or שלהן

TIP
The use of the masculine plural instead of feminine plural is quite common. So שלהם *theirs* and שלכם *our*, can be used instead of שלהן and שלכן.

ADJECTIVES

02.03 Listen and repeat the following adjectives, divided into masculine and feminine, singular and plural:

	beautiful				big				small			
m/s	יפה	יפה	יפה	**yafe**	גדול	גדול	**gadol**	קטן	קטן	**katan**
f/s	יפה	יפה	יפה	**yafa**	גדולה	גדולה	**gdola**	קטנה	קטנה	**ktana**
m/p	יפים	יפים	יפים	**yafim**	גדולים	גדולים	**gdolim**	קטנים	קטנים	**ktanim**
f/p	יפות	יפות	יפות	**yafot**	גדולות	גדולות	**gdolot**	קטנות	קטנות	**ktanot**

	tall				short				slim			
m/s	**gavoha**	גבוה	גבוה	**namuch**	נמוך	נמוך	**raze**	רזה	רזה
f/s	**gvohaa**	גבוהה	גבוהה	**nemucha**	נמוכה	נמוכה	**raza**	רזה	רזה
m/p	**gvohim**	גבוהים	גבוהים	**nemuchim**	נמוכים	נמוכים	**razim**	רזים	רזים
f/p	**gvohot**	גבוהות	גבוהות	**nemuchot**	נמוכות	נמוכות	**razot**	רזות	רזות

You have already learned that feminine nouns in the singular form usually end with ה, and in the plural they usually end with ת. You have also learned that masculine nouns in the plural usually end with ים. See if you can apply this rule to the adjective for *beautiful*: יפה.

TIP
In Hebrew, the opposite meaning of an adjective can be expressed by simply adding *not* לא **lo** before the word. For example, the opposite of *beautiful* is expressed as *not beautiful* יפה **yafe/yafa**, so לא יפה **lo yafe/lo yafa**.

Conversation and comprehension 2

David shows a picture of his family to Rachel. Pay attention to the difference between the pronunciation of the name 'Rachel' in English and in Hebrew, then answer the following question.

1 What does David's mother look like?

David	zo hamishpacha sheli.	זו המשפחה שלי.
Rachel	mishpacha gdola veyafa.	משפחה גדולה ויפה.
David	ken, aba, ima, bat, ben, saba, savta.	כן, אבא, אימא, בת, בן, סבא, סבתא.
Rachel	eifo ata batmuna?	איפה אתה בתמונה?
David	ze ani.	זה אני.
Rachel	mi zo?	מי זו?
David	zo ima sheli.	זו אימא שלי.
Rachel	ima shelcha gvoha veyafa.	אימא שלך גבוהה ויפה.
David	ken, ima sheli yafa.	כן, אימא שלי יפה.
Rachel	ima shelcha gvoha?	אימא שלך גבוהה?
David	lo, ima sheli nemucha veraza.	לא, אימא שלי נמוכה ורזה.

> **TIP**
> Take note of the how the definite article is contracted with the infinitive when Rachel asks, *Where are you in the picture?* איפה אתה בַּתמונה? **Eifo ata batmuna?** ב+ה = בַּ. The vowel in the letter *bet* would change if it was an indefinite article. So if Rachel were to ask, *Where are you in a picture?* she would say איפה אתה בְּתמונה? **Eifo ata betmuna?** ב+ה= בְּ.

2 Mark the following words from the conversation according to whether they are masculine or feminine, or singular or plural. Remember the rule about the use of feminine and masculine in the plural.

  a תמונה
  b משפחות
  c סבא
  d אבא
  e אימא
  f רזות
  g תלמידים

3 02.05 **Listen and repeat the following phrases that incorporate descriptive words. Make sure that you pay attention to difficult sounds.**

נמוך/ אני זו /אני זה/ גבוה/ וסבתא סבא/ קטנה תמונה/ גדולה משפחה/ יפה אימא

 02.06 *Listen to the following conversation. What is Grandma asking David?*

David	boker tov, ma shlomchem?	בוקר טוב, מה שלומכם?
Saba	tov toda. ve-atem?	טוב, תודה. ואתם?
David	tov meod.	טוב מאוד.
Saba	ata talmid tov?	אתה תלמיד טוב?
David	ken, saba.	כן, סבא.
Saba	ata ben katan ve-tov.	אתה בן קטן וטוב.
Savta	ata rotze kafe?	אתה רוצה קפה?
David	ken, meod, toda.	כן, מאוד, תודה.

In the conversation the grandfather asks: *and you?* (?ואתם). In the first unit you learned a list of connectives.

You have also learned the pronouns (*I, you*). These words are very important in any language. Try and memorize them, then answer the following questions.

3 **If Ruth visits her grandparents, how will her grandmother ask if she wants some coffee?**

4 **Answer the questions.**
   a When does David visit his grandparents?
   b Who offers coffee?
   c Is David a good pupil?

6 02.07 **Listen and repeat the following questions, paying close attention to the difference between masculine and feminine words.**

Feminine	transliteration	Masculine	Transliteration
את בת?	At bat?	אתה בן?	Ata ben?
יש לך משפחה גדולה?	Yesh lach mishpacha gdola?	יש לך משפחה גדולה?	Yesh lecha mishpacha gdola?
איפה את גרה?	Eifo at gara?	איפה אתה גר?	Eifo ata gar?
בת כמה את?	Bat kama at?	בן כמה אתה?	Ben kama ata?
את נמוכה?	At nemucha?	אתה נמוך?	Ata namuch?

Learn more

Hebrew verbs have roots which are mostly three letters in length, and are very helpful tools for learning the language.

	m/s	f/s	m/p	f/p
לרצות **lirzot** *to want*	רוצה **rotze** *wants*	רוצה **rotza** *wants*	רוצים **rotzim** *want*	רוצות **rotzot** *want*
להבין **lehavin** to understand	מבין **mevin**	מבינה **mevina**	מבינים **mevinim**	מבינות **mevinot**
לנסוע **linsoa** to go	נוסע **nosea**	נוסעת **nosaat**	נוסעים **noseem**	נוסעות **nosot**
לגור **lagur** to live (somewhere)	גר **gar**	גרה **gara**	גרים **garim**	גרות **garot**
לדבר **ledaber** to speak	מדבר **medaber**	מ_____ת **medaberet**	מ_____ים **medabrim**	מ_____ות **medabrot**

1 **Can you add the root of the verb** *to speak* לדבר **to the table?**
2 **How does the verb** *to live* **differ from the other verbs?**

3 **Now it is your turn to answer these questions about your own family.**

a ?המשפחה שלך גדולה hamishpacha shelcha (s/m) / shelach (f/m) gdola?

b ?אימא שלך יפה Ima shelach (s/f) shelcha (s/m) yafa?

c ?יש לך תמונה של המשפחה שלכם Yesh lecha(s/m) / yesh lach(s/f) tmuna shel hamishpacha shelacem?

 Reading and writing

1 **Write down the pronoun which relates to who is described in each sentence.**

a אבא של אבא aba shel aba _____

b בן של אבא ben shel aba _____

c בת של אימא bat shel ima _____

d בת של סבתא bat shel savta _____

e בת של סבא bat shel saba _____

2 **Choose the correct adjective from the options given in brackets.**

a אבא (זה / זו)

b סבא לא (גר / גרה) בתל-אביב

c משפחה (גדולה / גדולים)

d דן (בן / בת) 20

e תמונה לא (יפה / יפות)

3 **Choose the correct inflection of the following words and phrases from the options given in brackets.**

a הבת (נמוך / נמוכה)

b יש לי תמונה (קטן / קטנה)

c הבן שלי (גדול / גדולה)

d סבא (גר / גרה)

20

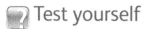# Test yourself

Translate the following passage into English. Use the transliteration if you need it and go back and look at the vocabulary earlier in the unit for help.

המשפחה שלי משפחה גדולה: אבא, אימא, 2 סבים ו-2 סבתות. יש לי 2 אחים ו-3 אחיות. האחים שלי גבוהים ויפים, והאחיות שלי נמוכות ויפות.	Hamishpacha sheli gdola: aba, ima, 2 sabim ve 2 savtot. Yesh li 2 achim ve 3 achayot. Haachim sheli gvohim veyafim, vehaachayot sheli nemuchot veyafot.

SELF CHECK

I CAN...
● ...ask and answer how someone is.
● ...describe myself and my family members.
● ...describe a person's appearance.
● ...correctly use the possessive forms.
● ...conjugate masculine and feminine verbs into the present tense.

Staying in a hotel

In this unit you will learn how to:
▶ *make a hotel reservation.*
▶ *express personal preferences.*
▶ *spell personal information.*
▶ *provide a telephone number.*

CEFR *(A1): Can ask people for things, give information and handle numbers, quantities, cost and time.*

Exploring places of interest

Israel is only a small country, but is rich in beautiful landscapes and heritage sites. Tel-Aviv תל-אביב is in the mid-west of the country and is Israel's financial and cultural capital. It is on the seafront and is known as 'the city that never sleeps' because of the cosmopolitan lifestyle of its residents. If you take a stroll along the חוף **chof**, you can take in the atmosphere of the many cafés, bars and restaurants. Enjoy traditional Israeli street food with a falafel from one of the many famous stands on Dizengoff Street דיזנגוף or take in the culture at the theatres, opera and concert halls. If you stay in a מלון **malon** near the sought-after beachfront, you will be in close proximity to Jaffa, which has a rich variety of old buildings, art galleries and fish restaurants.

Jerusalem is a worldwide focus of interest. It is the holy city to the three monotheistic religions of Islam, Judaism and Christianity. About an hour's drive from a hotel in Jerusalem will take you to the Dead Sea, as well as to Masada. Though the south of the country is mostly desert, you can enjoy attractions such as Beer-Sheba, the Ramon crater. The most southern tip of Israel is Eilat. It is on the Red Sea and has beaches, coral reef and a large choice of hotels.

Can you read the Hebrew signposts to these well-known cities?

אילת   מצרת   ירושלים   תל-אביב   חיפה

Vocabulary builder

03.01 **Listen and repeat the following words and complete the missing examples. You might want to pay particular attention to practising the pronunciation of** *to send* לִשְׁלוֹחַ **lishloach.**

מלון	מלון	malon	_____
חדר	חדר	cheder	room
חדר זוגי	חדר זוגי	cheder zugi	double room
הזמנה	הזמנה	hazmana	reservation / order
מזגן	מזגן	mazgan	air-conditioner
אמבטיה או מקלחת	אמבטיה או מקלחת	ambatia / miklachat	bath / shower
מתי	מתי	matay	when
מ...עה...	מ...עד...	me ... ad	from ... until
עם	עם	im	with
יום / ימים	יום / ימים	yom / yamim	day / days
להזמין	להזמין	lehazmin	to order
לבקש	לבקש	levakesh	to ask for
לשלוח	לשלוח	lishloach	to send
תאריך	תאריך	taarich	date
שירותים בחדר	שירותים בחדר	sherutim bacheder	en suite
ללא עישון	ללא עישון	lelo ishun	non smoking
טלפון	טלפון	telephon	_____
מייל	מייל	email	_____
טלביזייה	טלביזיה	televizia	_____
בר	בר	bar	bar

>
> The Hebrew word for *bath* אמבטיה **ambatia** is derived from the Greek word **embate**.

1 **How would you say** *in the hotel* **and** *in the room*?

2 **How do you say** *or* **in Hebrew?**

3 **How do you say** *a room with an air-conditioner*?

NUMBERS AND GENDER

The gender used for numbers is determined by the gender of the accompanying noun.

	Male		Female	
1	אחד	**echad**	אחת	**achat**
2	שניים	**shnayim**	שתיים	**shtayim**
3	שלושה	**shlosha**	שלוש	**shalosh**
4	ארבעה	**arbaa**	ארבע	**arba**
5	חמישה	**chamisha**	חמש	**chamesh**
6	שישה	**shisha**	שש	**shesh**
7	שבעה	**shiva**	שבע	**sheva**
8	שמונה	**shmona**	שמונֶה	**shmone**
9	תשעה	**tisha**	תשע	**tesha**
10	עשרה	**asara**	עשר	**eser**

> **TIP**
> Zero in Hebrew is אפס **efes** and is gender neutral.

 # Conversation and comprehension

03.02 *Dan wants to book a room in the Hilton hotel. He calls the hotel to check availability.*

1 For how many days will Dan stay in the hotel?

Hotel receptionist	Malon Hilton, shalom.	מלון הילטון, שלום.
Dan	Shalom. Ani mevakesh lehazmin cheder.	אני מבקש להזמין חדר.
Receptionist	Matay?	מתי?
Dan	Mishlosha ad asara beyuni.	משלושה עד עשרה ביוני.
Receptionist	Tov.	טוב.
Dan	Hacheder gadol o katan?	החדר גדול או קטן?
Receptionist	Hacheder gadol, veyesh sherutim bacheder, telephone vetelevizia.	החדר גדול, ויש שירותים בחדר, טלפון וטלוויזיה.
Dan	Yesh miklachat o ambatia?	יש מקלחת או אמבטיה?
Receptionist	Yesh ambatia.	יש אמבטיה.
Dan	Toda lach.	תודה לך.
Receptionist	Toda lecha!	תודה לך!

2 Which words in the conversation are similar to words in English?

3 Describe in English the type of room Dan will get.

4 What is the gender of the operator?

 Language discovery

1 Find the expressions that mean the following:
  a I ask for
  b to order

2 Translate the following conjunctions:
  a ו **ve**
  b או **o**
  c מ **me**

3 Practise your genders, and read the last conversation as Ruth calling the hotel instead of Dan.

VERBS

to order	להזמין	*להזמין*	lehazmin
(m/s)	מזמין	*מזמין*	mazmin
(f/s)	מזמינה	*מזמינה*	mazmina
(m/p)	מזמינים	*מזמינים*	mazminim
(f/p)	מזמינות	*מזמינות*	mazminot
to ask for	לבקש	*לבקש*	levakesh
(m/s)	מבקש	*מבקש*	mevakesh
(f/s)	מבקשת	*מבקשת*	mevakeshet
(m/p)	מבקשים	*מבקשים*	mevakshim
(f/p)	מבקשות	*מבקשות*	mevakshot
to send	לשלוח	*לשלוח*	lishloach
(m/s)	שולח	*שולח*	sholeach
(f/s)	שולחת	*שולחת*	sholachat
(m/p)	שולחים	*שולחים*	sholchim
(f/p)	שולחות	*שולחות*	sholchot

> **TIP**
> The roots appear in other related words. For instance, the root בקש from *ask for* appears in similar words like: *request, wanted* and *application*.

4 **Complete the following sentences with the Hebrew verbs you have just learned.**

  a Dan _____ an e-mail.

  b David and Ron _____ to order a room.

  c Ruth _____ a cup of coffee.

  d I _____ some groceries from the supermarket.

  e Ruth and Rachel _____ letters to each other.

> **TIP**
>
> In Israel mobile phone numbers have a three-digit area code while regular telephones have a two-digit area code.

5 **Read these telephone numbers in Hebrew:**

14 6732588; 250 6325912; 38 9456223; 454 6923156; 58 9067317

6 **You need to make a hotel reservation using the Hebrew you have just learned.**

  a Ask for a single room, for six days, with bath, television and a bar.

  b Ask if the room is small or big.

  c Ask for a non-smoking room.

  d Give your phone number.

  e Ask if there is coffee in the room.

  f Ask if there is a television in the room.

7 **Use the Hebrew verbs you already know to complete these sentences.**

  a I don't (understand) _____ the operator.

  b She (works) _____ in a hotel

  c We (want) _____ a non-smoking room.

  d He (sends) _____ an e-mail.

  e Do you (ask for) _____ a big room.

  f I don't (speak) _____ Hebrew.

ANTONYMS

Remember that you can add the word *not* לא before the verb, and invert its meaning. For example, the verb *work* עובד **oved** becomes *does not work* לא עובד **lo oved**.

8 Revise the vocabulary at the start of the unit. Now see if you can say the opposite of the following:

a	יש	Yesh	**e**	יפה	Yafe
b	מזמין	Mazmin	**f**	רוצה	Rotze
c	מבין	Mevin	**g**	מדבר	Medaber
d	שולח	Shole'ach	**h**	גדול	Gadol

 ## Practice

 1 03.03 **Listen and repeat the following phrases.**

החדר הזה יפה	**hacheder haze yafe**
החדר לא יפה	**hacheder loyafe**
הוא מזמין חדר לשמונה ימים	**hoo mazmin cheder leshmona yamim**
אין בחדר טלוויזיה	**ein bacheder televizia**
מה המייל שלך?	**ma hamail shelach?**

2 **Now answer these questions.**

a אתה גר במלון?	ata gar bamalon?
b אתה רוצה לגור במלון?	ata rotze lagur bemalon?
c מתי אתה רוצה לטייל?	matay ata rotze letayel?

> **TIP**
> The expression *no vacancy* does not exist in Hebrew, instead we use the combination *no vacant room*.

You have learned the word נעים מאוד. מאוד means 'very pleased to meet you'.

sorry	מצטער	miztaer	
(m/s)	מזמין	מזמין	mitztaer
(f/s)	מזמינה	מזמינה	mitztaeret
(m/p)	מזמינים	מזמינים	mitztaarim
(f/p)	מזמינות	מזמינות	mitztaarot

Reading and writing

USEFUL LANGUAGE

מצטער	מצטער	Mitztaer	sorry
פנוי	פנוי	Panuy	vacant
מאוד	מאד	Meod	very

You are just about to check in to your hotel room. Can you fill in your own personal details, the dates you want to stay and your room requirements?

תאריך:_____

שם:_____

מ_____ עד _____

בחדר:_____

 Test yourself

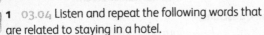

1 03.04 Listen and repeat the following words that are related to staying in a hotel.

מסעדה	**misada**	restaurant
בר	**bar**	bar
קבל	**kabala**	reception
חדרים	**chadarim**	rooms
מעלית	**maalit**	lift
מכון כושר	**machon kosher**	gym
בריכת שחייה	**breichat schiya**	swimming pool
קומה	**koma**	floor

2 Complete the sentences using the words provided in the box.

מצטער, להזמין, מבקש, מתי, לא עובד, מאוד, לשלוח

a I want to _____ a take-away pizza.

b Do you _____ for a cup of coffee?

c I am going _____ a letter to my aunt.

d I went on holiday for eight _____.

e _____ are you going to visit us?

f He is unemployed, he _____.

g _____, I don't know.

h I love you _____ much.

SELF CHECK

I CAN. . .
○ . . . make a hotel reservation.
● . . . understand phone messages.
● . . . read numbers from 1 to 10.
● . . . read and complete an application form.
○ . . . express my personal preferences.

Review units 1–3

MASCULINE AND FEMININE FORMS

1 **Do you remember the rule of how to identify feminine and masculine nouns? Try and identify these nouns as masculine singular or plural, or feminine singular or plural.**

a משפחה

b תמונה

c חדרים

d הזמנות

e תאריך

f בנות

g אח

h טלפונים

i אחות

j טלביזיה

2 **Do you remember the rules of adjective forms? Write down the forms of these adjectives that agree with the following nouns.**

a _____ תמונות (יפה)

b _____ בנות (רזה)

c _____ מלון (קטן)

d _____ חדרים (קטן)

e _____ טלביזיה (גדול)

f _____ חדר (פנוי)

3 **You have learned about possessive pronouns. Now translate the following words into Hebrew.**

a my

b your (m/s)

c your (f/s)

d his

e her

f our

g your (m/p)

h your (f/p)

i their (m/p)

j their (f/p)

NUMBERS

4 Practise reading out the following numbers in Hebrew

12 / 6 / 9 / 3 / 20 / 13 / 1 / 18 / 4 / 15 / 7 / 20

PERSONAL PRONOUNS

5 Can you match these Hebrew and English personal pronouns?

a	I	**1**	הן
b	you (m/s)	**2**	אני
c	you (f/s)	**3**	אתה
d	he	**4**	הוא
e	she	**5**	אנחנו
f	we	**6**	את
g	you (m/p)	**7**	היא
h	you (f/p)	**8**	אתם
i	they (m/p)	**9**	הם
j	they (f/p)	**10**	אתן

VERBS

6 You have learned the forms of verbs in the masculine and feminine singular and plural. Now follow the example and complete the verbs, filling in the missing words.

m/s	גר	מזמין	מדבר	מבקש	מבין
f/s	גרה	מזמינ_____	_____	_____	_____
m/p	גרים	מזמינ_____	_____	_____	_____
f/p	גרות	מזמינ_____	_____	_____	_____

7 Translate from Hebrew to English.

a אנחנו מדברים עברית

b דן נוסע מתל-אביב לירושלים

c ?אתה רוצה תה או קפה

d החדרים שלנו גדולים

e אימא שלי יפה

8 Translate from English to Hebrew.

a I understand English.

b My family lives in Tel-Aviv.

c This room is beautiful.

d We have a big family.

e My email is …

Shopping

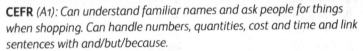

In this unit you will learn:
▶ *prices and quantities.*
▶ *numbers from ten to 100.*
▶ *to ask for help when shopping.*
▶ *to review and express preferences.*
▶ *the names for articles of clothing and shoes.*
▶ *adjectives for clothes and measurement.*

CEFR *(A1): Can understand familiar names and ask people for things when shopping. Can handle numbers, quantities, cost and time and link sentences with and/but/because.*

Israeli fashion

Israeli fashion today is fresh and bold, with designers such as Ronen Chen and Kedem Sasson. This was not always the case, however, and the history of clothing in Israel from the end of the 19th century onwards has been as changeable as Israel's society and culture.

As in every culture, Israeli fashion reflects the socio-political sentiment of the people. The early Jewish settlers were fashion pioneers and adopted a 'retro' Oriental look, inspired by biblical pictures. The Socialist pioneers, who established the **Kibbutz** קיבוץ settlements, wore worn-out clothes and the Bedouin head cover, called **keffiyeh** כפייה. This desire to leave Europe אירופה behind and find new means of self-expression grew after the holocaust.

After a period of decline in the Israeli fashion industry as a result of wars and western influences, young, new designers have started to become more popular. In 2011 Tel-Aviv תל-אביב held its first fashion week in almost 20 years עשרים **esrim**, with special guest, the Italian designer, Roberto Cavalli.

Can you guess what the Hebrew words would be for *t-shirt* **and** *jeans***?**

Vocabulary builder

 04.01 **Listen and repeat these words which relate to shopping.**

יקר	יָקָר	yakar	*expensive*
זול	זוֹל	zol	*cheap*
מחיר	מְחִיר	mechir	*price*
מידה	מִידָה	mida	*size*
מכנסיים	מִכְנָסַיִים	michnasayim	*trousers*
חולצה	חוּלְצָה	chultza	*shirt (blouse)*
שמלה	שִׂמְלָה	simla	*dress*
חליפה	חֲלִיפָה	chalifa	*suit*

SINGULAR NOUNS (M/F)

1 **The words listed above are in singular masculine and feminine forms. Can you find the equivalent singular form of these nouns in the following list?**

חנויות, מחירים, שמלות, חולצות

TAKE A MOMENT TO REMEMBER

▶ You learned in the first lesson that verb endings for singular and feminine words regularly end with ה, or ת.

▶ Feminine plural verbs regularly end with וֹת.

▶ Masculine plural verbs usually end with ים.

▶ The same rules apply to nouns.

2 **Can you see the connection between these words?**

משקפיים glasses; נעליים shoes; גרביים socks; שניים – שתיים two

NEW EXPRESSIONS

 04.02 **Listen and repeat these new expressions.**

כמה זה עולה?	כַּמָה זֶה עוֹלֶה?	Kama ze ole?	*How much does it cost?*
אני מעדיף	אֲנִי מַעֲדִיף	Ani maadif (m)	*I prefer*
אני מעדיפה	אֲנִי מַעֲדִיפָה	Ani maadifa (f)	*I prefer*
אני קונה	אֲנִי קוֹנֶה	Ani kone (m)	*I buy*
אני קונה	אֲנִי קוֹנָה	Ani kona (f)	*I buy*
זה יקר	זֶה יָקָר	Ze yakar.	*This is expensive.*
זה יקר מידי	זֶה יָקָר מִידִי	Ze yakar miday.	*This is too expensive.*
אפשר לעזור לך?	אֶפְשָׁר לַעֲזוֹר לָךְ?	Efshar laazor lach? (f) lecha? (m)	*May I help you?*

איזה מספר?	*איזה מספר?*	Eize (m) mispar?	What number?
איזו מידה?	*איזה איזו מידה?*	Eizo (f) mida?	What size?

Conversation and comprehension 1

04.03 *Mrs. Brown enters a clothing store. Listen to her conversation with the salesman.*

1 What does she think is too expensive?

Mr Lapid	Shalom, efshar laazor lach?	שלום, אפשר לעזור לך?
Mrs Brown	Shalom, ani rotza begged yafe.	שלום, אני רוצה בגד יפה.
Mr Lapid	At rotza michnasayim vechultza?	את רוצה מכנסיים וחולצה?
Mrs Brown	Lo, toda, ani maadifa simla.	לא, תודה, אני מעדיפה שמלה.
Mr Lapid	Zo simla yafa.	זו שמלה יפה.
Mrs Brown	Zo simla yafa, aval – lo, toda	זו שמלה יפה, אבל – לא, תודה.
Mr Lapid	Lama?	למה?
Mrs Brown	Ki hasimla yekara.	כי השמלה יקרה.
Mr Lapid	Vehasimla hazo?	והשמלה הזו?
Mrs Brown	Zo simla yafa vezola.	זו שמלה יפה וזולה.
Mr Lapid	Ze mat'im?	זה מתאים?
Mrs Brown	Ken, ze mat'im.	כן, זה מתאים.

2 Select the items of clothing Mrs Brown wants from the list.

יקרה, מכנסיים, חולצה, שמלה יפה, שמלה יפה חולה.

3 Did Mrs Brown find what she was looking for?

4 Does the dress fit her?

5 Match the Hebrew with the English.

a	יפה	1	I prefer (m)
b	זול	2	expensive
c	אני מעדיף	3	beautiful
d	אני מעדיפה	4	cheap
e	יקר	5	I prefer (f)

6 Match the questions to the answers.

a It costs 300 ₪.

b No, I prefer a long dress.

c It is not expensive.

d Yes this is size ...

1 ?את מעדיפה שמלה קצרה

2 ?זו מידה 44

3 ?כמה זה עולה

4 ?זה לא יקר

Learn more

NUMBERS 11–100 AND 101–1000

As you already know the numbers from 1 to 10, you will see that learning the numbers from 11 to 1000 is quite easy. The principle is: one + ten = אחת עשרה **achat esreh**. We will only use the female form of the numbers, as this is the preferred way to count in Hebrew. Later, you will use female and male numbers, according to the nouns that follow.

TIP

Hundreds are expressed in the plural: שלוש מאות **shlosh meot** (f).

If you look carefully you will find some common denominations between male and female numbers.

11	אחד עשר	אחד עשר	achad asar (m)
	אחת עשרה	אחת עשרה	achat esreh (f)
12	שנים עשר	שנים עשר	shneim asar (m)
	שתים עשרה	שתים עשרה	shteim esreh (f)
13	שלושה עשר	שלושה עשר	shlosha asar (m)
	שלוש עשרה	שלוש עשרה	shlosh esreh (f)
14	ארבעה עשר	ארבעה עשר	arbaa asar (m)
	ארבע עשרה	ארבע עשרה	arba esreh (f)
15	חמישה עשר	חמישה עשר	chamisha asar (m)
	חמש עשרה	חמש עשרה	chamesh esreh (f)

16	שישה עשר	*handwriting*	chamisha asar (m)
	שש עשרה	*handwriting*	shesh esreh (f)
17	שבעה עשר	*handwriting*	shiv'ah asar (m)
	שבע עשרה	*handwriting*	shva esreh (f)
18	שמונה עשר	*handwriting*	shmona asar (m)
	שמונה עשרה	*handwriting*	shmoneh esreh (f)
19	תשעה עשר	*handwriting*	tish'ah asar (m)
	תשע עשרה	*handwriting*	tsha esreh (f)
20	עשרים	*handwriting*	esrim (m, f)

1 Write down the numbers between 10 and 100.

a שש עשרה שמלות   _____ dresses

b ארבע עשרה חולצות   _____ shirts

c תשעה עשר בגדים   _____ clothes

d עשרים חנויות   _____ shops

e שתים עשרה חליפות   _____ suits

2 Review your answers and see how many of these numbers you can remember from the conversation between Mrs Brown and Mr Lapid.

100	מאה	*handwriting*	meah
200	מאתיים	*handwriting*	matayim
300	שלוש מאות	*handwriting*	shlosh meot
400	ארבע מאות	*handwriting*	arba meot
500	חמש מאות	*handwriting*	chamesh meot
600	שש מאות	*handwriting*	shesh meot
700	שבע מאות	*handwriting*	shva meot
800	שמונה מאות	*handwriting*	shmone meot
900	תשע מאות	*handwriting*	tsha meot
1000	אלף	*handwriting*	elef

TIP

Remember you learned that *and* in Hebrew is ו **ve**.

3 Translate the numbers. The first one has been done for you.

a מאתיים עשרים ושתים   222

b מאה וחמש עשרה   _____

c ארבע מאות שלושים ושנתיים   _____

d תשע מאות שבעים ושתים   _____

e שבע מאות שמונים וחמש   _____

f מאה אלף עשרים וחמש   _____

TIP

The number 301 will be שלוש מאות ואחת **shlosh meot ve'achat.**

Practice

צבעים *TZVA'IM COLOURS*

04.04 **Listen and repeat these colour words.**

צבעים	צבעים	tzva'im	*colours*
שחור	שחור	shachor	*black*
לבן	לבן	lavan	*white*
ירוק	ירוק	yarok	*green*
כחול	כחול	kachol	*blue*
אדום	אדום	adom	*red*
צהוב	צהוב	tzahov	*yellow*

When used as an adjective, colours are inflected according to the gender of the noun.

gender	black	white	green	blue	red	yellow
m/s	שחור	לבן	ירוק	כחול	אדום	צהוב
f/s	שחורה	לבנה	ירוקה	כחולה	אדומה	צהובה
m/p	שחורים	לבנים	ירוקים	כחולים	אדומים	צהובים
f/p	שחורות	לבנות	ירוקות	כחולות	אדומות	צהובות

> **TIP**
>
> In the exercises that follow you will practise masculine and feminine plural adjectives. Remember that when we count we use the feminine form.

1 04.05 **Listen and repeat the following sentences, and try to translate them into English. Take note of the difference between the masculine and feminine forms.**

   a Ani rotze / rotza chultza tzehuba   אני רוצה / רוצה חולצה צהובה

   b Hasimla ktzara miday   השמלה קצרה מידי

   c Hasimla ola 400 shekel   השמלה עולה 400 שקל

   d Hachalifa zola   החליפה זולה

2 **Write down the correct numbers.**

   a שלוש מאות   **e** מאתיים ואחת

   b מאה עשרים וחמש   **f** ארבע

   c חמש עשרה   **g** שלוש עשרה

   d שבע   **h** עשרים ושבע

3 04.06 **Listen to the questions in Hebrew and provide your own answers in English. Remember** *your (m)* = **shelcha and** *your (f)* = **shelach.**

a ‏איזה צבע יפה?‏

b ‏אתה רוצה מכנסיים יקרים או זולים?‏

c ‏אתם רוצים לקנות בגדים?‏

d ‏מה המידה שלך?‏

 # Conversation and comprehension 2

04.07 A mother and her son enter a clothes shop. How many items of clothing do they buy?

Mother	Ata rotze michnasayim levanim?	‏אתה רוצה מכנסיים לבנים?‏
Son	Lo, ani rotze michnasayim kchulim.	‏לא, אני רוצה מכנסיים כחולים.‏
Mother	O.K. jeans?	‏או, קי, ג'ינס?‏
Son	Ken, jeans.	‏כן, ג'ינס.‏
Mother	Eizo chultza?	‏איזו חולצה?‏
Son	Shtey chultzot?	‏שתי חולצות?‏
Mother	O.K., Eize tzvaim?	‏או קי, איזה צבעים?‏
Son	Tzahov veadom	‏צהוב ואדום.‏
Mother	Ze mat'im?	‏זה מתאים ?‏
Son	Ken, ze mat'im, toda.	‏כן, זה מתאים, תודה.‏

1 **The mother agrees to buy the clothes. How would you say this in Hebrew?**

2 **How many colours are mentioned in the conversation?**

PARTICLES REINFORCEMENT

‏כי‏	*כי*	**ki**	*because*
‏אבל‏	*אבל...*	**aval**	*but*
‏ו...‏	*...ו*	**ve**	*and*
‏עם‏	*עם*	**im**	*with*

TIP
In Hebrew instead of *OK* you can say *good* ‏טוב‏, **tov**.

38

4 **Translate the following sentences. You can use a dictionary and the glossary to help you.**

a Salesman: _____ ?אפשר לעזור לך

b Salesman: _____ ?איזו מידה מתאימה

c Customer: _____ אני מעדיף חולצה לבנה

d Customer: _____ ?כמה זה עולה

e Customer: _____ אני מבקשת שתי חולצות זולות

f Customer: _____ אני לא קונה, כי זה יקר מידי

g Customer: _____ .אימא קונה בגדים עם דן

Practice

1 **Conjugate the adjectives. They relate to clothes shopping.**

adjective	m/s	f/s	m/p	f/p
fit	מתאים	מתאימה	מתאימים	מתאימות
big	גדול		גדולים	
small		קטנה	קטנים	
short	קצר			קצרות
long			ארוכים	ארוכות
cheap	זול		זולים	זולות
expensive		יקרה	יקרים	

2 **Complete the following sentences with one of the Hebrew colours listed below. Note that some colours are repeated.**

לבן שחור שווד כחול צהובה ירוק קורק אדום

a The sea is _____.

b The grass is _____.

c When the traffic lights are _____ stop!

d The sun is _____ (f/s).

e _____ as night.

f The colours of the Israeli flag are _____ and _____.

3 **You are going on a business trip and need to buy some essential items of clothing. Write out a shopping list, then estimate the cost of the items.**

TIP

סוף עונה (**sof ona**) *end of season,* means *discounts.*

Go further

Read the following colours and colour-related words.

	pink	grey	orange	turquoise
m/s	ורוד **varod**	אפור **afor**	כתום **katom**	טורקיז **turquoise**
f/s	ורודה **vruda**	אפורה **afora**	כתומה **ktuma**	טורקיז **turquoise**
m/p	ורודים **vrudim**	אפורים **aforim**	כתומים **ktumim**	טורקיז **turquoise**
f/p	ורודות **vrudot**	אפורות **aforot**	כתומות **ktumot**	טורקיז **turquoise**
	light	*dark*		
m/s	בהיר **bahir**	כהה **kehe**		
f/s	בהירה **behira**	כהה **keha**		
m/p	בהירים **behirim**	כהים **kehim**		
f/p	בהירות **behirot**	כהות **kehot**		

> **TIP**
> When a colour is used as a noun, it is referred to in the masculine singular.

> **TIPS**
> - As you know, when a colour is used as an adjective, it takes the gender of the nouns which follow. For example: חולצה לבנה **chultzah levanah** (f/s).
> - As *turquoise* is a Latin word, it remains the same whether it is used as a noun or as an adjective.
> - The accentuation is on the last vowel of the word.

Test yourself

Translate the following into English.

1 זה עולה חמש מאות שקל. Ze ole chamesh meot shekel.

2 חמישים + עשרים = ? Esrim + chamishim = ?

3 החליפה הירוקה יפה. Hachalifa hayeruka yafa.

4 החולצה הכחולה מתאימה. Hachultza hakchula mat'uma.

5 בסוף העונה הבגדים זולים. Besof ona habegadim zolim.

40

SELF CHECK

I CAN...

- ○ ...count from one to 1000.
- ○ ...name the colours in Hebrew.
- ○ ...inflect adjectives.
- ○ ...link sentences with *and*, *but*, *because* and practise grammar.
- ○ ...express opinions on colours, preferences, sizes and prices.
- ○ ...successfully go shopping for clothes!

Travelling

In this unit you will learn how to:
- ▶ *identify means of transport and words for directions.*
- ▶ *enquire about bus, plane, train timetables and buy tickets.*
- ▶ *tell the time.*
- ▶ *identify the days of the week and hours in the day.*

CEFR *(A1): Can get travel recommendations, and ask relevant questions to travel by bus, train, plane and car. Can also understand a timetable, and ask for tickets and directions.*

The Israeli flag

As your plane touches down at Ben-Gurion Airport בן-גוריון שדה תעופה, one of the first things you will encounter is a waving Israeli flag. This flag was adopted as the national symbol in 1948, the year in which the State of Israel מדינת ישראל (**Medinat Yisrael)** was established. The background of the flag is לבן, with two horizontal blue כחול (**kachol)** stripes and a blue hexagram, called a מגן דויד (**Magen David)**, or Star of David in its centre. The basic design of the flag is inspired by the טלית (**Talit)**, the Jewish prayer shawl.

The Star of David was discovered in ornamentation found in antique synagogues dating back to the time of the second temple. It was only adopted as a Jewish symbol of identity from the Middle Ages onwards, by the Jews of Prague.

The national ambulance, disaster and emergency service in Israel is known as the 'Red Star of David'. Can you guess the Hebrew name for this?

Vocabulary builder

GETTING AROUND

 05.01 **Listen and repeat these new words relating to travel.**

אוטובוס	אוטובוס	autobus	bus
רכבת	רכבת	rakevet	train
מכונית	מכונית	mechonit	car
אוטו	אוטו	oto	automobile
טקסי	טקסי	taxi	taxi
מטוס	מטוס	matos	aeroplane
כרטיס	כרטיס	kartis	ticket
קופה	קופה	kupa	ticket office
מודיעין	מודיעין	modieen	information bureau
לוח-זמנים	לוח-זמנים	luach zmanim	timetable
זמן	זמן	zman	time
שעה	שעה	sha'a	hour
דקה	דקה	daka	minute
שבוע	שבוע	shavua	week
נהג	נהג	nehag	driver
רישיון נהיגה	רישיון נהיגה	rishyon nehiga	driving licence
לשכור	לשכור	liskor	to hire
לנהוג	לנהוג	linhog	to drive
לנסוע	לנסוע	linsoa	to go (by car / train)
לטוס	לטוס	latus	to fly
שדה תעופה	שדה תעופה	sde-teufa	airport
תחנה	תחנה	tachana	station
רציף	רציף	ratzif	platform

Look at the similarities between the words you have just learned and answer the following questions.

    a Identify the Hebrew word for time in לוח-זמנים (*timetable*)?

    b Find the word for driving in רישיון נהיגה (*driving licence*)?

    c Which letters are common to both aeroplane מטוס and pilot טייס?

    d Find three other words which are similar in both languages.

NEW EXPRESSIONS

...יוצאת מ (f)	יוֹצֵאת מ...	yotzet me...(f)	leaves from...
...יוצא מ (m)	יוֹצֵא מ...	yotze me...(m)	(place)
...מגיעה ל (f)	מַגִּיעָה ל...	magiah le...(f)	arrives in...
...מגיע ל (m)	מַגִּיעַ ל...	magia le...(m)	(place)
...יוצאת ב (f)	יוֹצֵאת ב...	yotzet be...(f)	leaves at...
...יוצא ב (m)	יוֹצֵא ב...	yotze be...(m)	(time)
...מגיעה ב (f)	מַגִּיעָה ב...	magiah be...(f)	arrives at...
...מגיע ב (m)	מַגִּיעַ ב...	magia be...(m)	(time)
?איפה	אֵיפֹה?	eifo?	where?
?לאן	לְאָן?	lean?	where to?
?מתי	מָתַי?	matay?	when?
?כמה זמן זה לוקח	כַּמָּה זְמַן זֶה לוֹקֵחַ?	kama zman ze lokeach?	How much time does it take?
הלוך ושוב	הָלוֹךְ וָשׁוֹב	haloch vashov	return ticket
כל שעה	כָּל שָׁעָה	kol shah	every hour
נסיעה טובה	נְסִיעָה טוֹבָה	nesiah tova	bon voyage

Conversation and comprehension 1

05.02 *Mr and Mrs Green are going on a bus journey. They enter the station and approach the information desk. Where are the Greens going?*

Clerk	Efshar laazor lachem?	אפשר לעזור לכם?
Mr Green	Anachnu rotzim linsoa leTel-Aviv.	אנחנו רוצים לנסוע לתל-אביב.
	Matay haotobus yotze?	מתי האוטובוס יוצא?
Clerk	Haotobus yotze beshaah shteim esreh.	האוטובוס יוצא בשעה שתים עשרה.
Mr Green	Eifo haotobus?	איפה האוטובוס?
Clerk	Beratzif shalosh.	ברציף שלוש.
Mrs Green	Todah.	תודה.
Clerk	Nesiah tova.	נסיעה טובה.

Mr and Mrs Green then go to the ticket office. What is the cost of a return fare?

Ticket officer	Efshar laazor lachem?	אפשר לעזור לכם?
Mrs Green	Kama ole kartis haloch vashov le Tel-Aviv?	כמה עולה כרטיס הלוך ושוב לתל-אביב?
Ticket officer	Arba'im vechameish shekels.	ארבעים וחמישה ש.
Mr Green	Shnayim bevakasha.	שניים בבקשה.
Ticket officer	Bevakasha.	בבקשה.
Mr Green	Toda.	תודה.

> **TIP**
> On your travels, you will see many אגד **eged**, *signs*. This is the name of the Israeli bus company. Public services such as telephones, lifts, escalators and toilets are all marked by these familiar icons.

1 **Can you repeat the three questions that the Greens ask the clerk?**

2 **On which platform is the bus standing?**

3 **At what time does the bus leave the station?**

4 **Match the English phrases with their Hebrew translations.**

a ?אפשר לעזור לך   **1** The bus leaves.

b כרטיס הלוך ושוב   **2** Bon voyage.

c רציף שלוש   **3** May I help you?

d האוטובוס יוצא   **4** Return ticket.

e נסיעה טובה   **5** Platform three.

 Language discovery

PARTICLES

When expressing the phrase *May I help you?* in Hebrew, it is easiest to first translate the English phrase to *Is it possible to help?* This literally translates to Hebrew as ל אפשר... **Efshar le...**

The same rule can be applied to other contexts. For example *May I travel to Jerusalem?* can be expressed as *Is it possible to travel to Jerusalem?*

1 **Complete the Hebrew sentences from the Hebrew examples given. Then try to give the full English translations.**

  1 אפשר *possible to ... (drive / travel)*

  2 ... ל רוצה

  3 ... ל... מ נוסע *travel from ... to ...*

  4 ... עד ...מ... *from ... to ... (time)*

  5 ... ב ... *eat ... (time)*

  6 -עד ... מ *from the ... until the ... (date)*

  a אני אוכל ב -7 בערב

  b רוצה לנסוע ?

  c מ. 10 עד 8-

  d באפריל 1 עד בינואר 3

  e נוסע מתל-אביב לירושלים

  f אפשר לנסוע ?לנהוג ?

TIME

Expressing units of time

חצי	*חצי*	Chetzi	Half
רבע	*רבע*	Reva	Quarter
שמונה וחצי	*שמונה וחצי*	Shmone iachetzi	Half past 8
ארבע ורבע	*ארבע ורבע*	Arba vareva	A quarter past 4
חמש שלושים	*חמש שלושים*	Chamesh shloshim	5 thirty
עשרים לעשר	*עשרים לעשר*	Esrim le'eser	twenty to 10
חמש דקות לשש	*חמש דקות לשש*	Chamesh dakot leshesh	5 minutes to 6

46

Here are a few examples of how you express time in Hebrew.

חמש דקות ל-שש	*five minutes to six*
שלוש ועשר דקות	*three and ten minutes*
רבע לשבע	*a quarter to seven*
רבע לשמונה	*a quarter to eight*
שמונה וחמש עשרה דקות	*eight fifteen*
חמש ורבע	*five fifteen*

TIP
Take note of how we use the words: to ...ל; & and ...ו

2 Give the correct time for the following:

DAYS OF THE WEEK

Days of the week are expressed as *Day* (**Yom**) followed by the number of the day. The week begins on Sunday, as **Shabbat** (*Saturday*) is the final day of the week.

יום ראשון	**Yom rishon**	*Sunday*
יום שני	**Yom Sheni**	*Monday*
יום שלישי	**Yom Shlishi**	*Tuesday*
יום רביעי	**Yom Reviee**	*Wednesday*
יום חמישי	**Yom Chamishi**	*Thursday*
יום שישי	**Yom Shishi**	*Friday*
שבת	**Shabbat**	*Saturday*

Practice

1 Translate the following phrases into Hebrew.
   a When (does) the train leave?
   b The taxi goes to Eilat.
   c The train arrives at the station.
   d Bon voyage!
   e Where is platform 3?
   f May I help you (m/s)?

2 Listen again to the Greens' conversations. Fill in the missing Hebrew words using the examples provided below.

קופה	מכונית (אוטו)	יצא	3	תל-אביב

   a The plane is _____ in the morning.
   b The train leaves from platform _____.
   c The bus goes to _____.
   d They buy their tickets at the _____.
   e I drive a _____.

> **TIP**
> You can use the word אוטו (**oto**) *automobile* when referring to your car, instead of using מכונית.

3 05.04 Listen to the description of Dan's travel plans.

   a From which airport does Dan's plane leave?

דן רוצה לטוס לאנגליה, ב – 10.7.11,
לשבעה ימים. הוא קונה כרטיס הלוך
-ושוב, ויוצא משדה התעופה "בן
גוריון", בשעה חמש בערב.

Dan rotze latus leanglia be- 10.7.11. le-shiv'a yamim. Hoo kone kartis haloch vashov, veyotze misde hateufa 'Ben-Gurion' beshaa chamesh baerev.

   b To which destination does Dan want to fly?
   c Did he buy a single or return ticket?
   d When does he leave the country, and when is he coming back?
   e What time does the flight leave?

Conversation and comprehension 2

05.05 *Ron and Dan would like to hire a car. Are they able to rent a car from the rental office?*

Clerk	Efshar la'azor lachem?	אפשר לעזור לכם?
Dan	Anachnu rotzim liskor mechonit.	אנחנו רוצים לשכור מכונית.
Clerk	Mechonit gdola o ktana?	מכונית גדולה או קטנה?
Dan	Mechonit ktana.	מכונית קטנה.
Clerk	Lekama zman?	לכמה זמן?
Dan	Leshavua. Kama ze ole?	לשבוע. כמה זה עולה?
Clerk	35 ₪ leyom. Mimatay ad maty?	שלושים וחמישה שקל ליום. ממתי עד מתי?
Dan	Me-1 beyanuar ad 7 beyanuar.	מ-אחד בינואר עד שבעה בינואר.
Clerk	Bevakasha.	בבקשה.
Dan	Toda.	תודה.

Now answer following questions.

a *How much does it cost?* is a useful phrase. How do you say it in Hebrew?

b *May I help you?* is another useful expression. Say it in Hebrew.

c For how long is the car hired?

d Do they ask for a big car, or a small one?

e How much does it cost?

 TIP

Take note of the common roots of nouns and verbs: נ.ס.ע/ נ.ה.ג/ ט.ו.ס.

noun

נהג	נֶהָג	nehag	driver
טייס	טַיִּיס	tayas	pilot
נוסע	נוֹסֵעַ	nosea	passenger

verb

לנהוג	לִנְהוֹג	linhog	to drive
לטוס	לָטוּס	latus	to fly
לנסוע	לִנְסוֹעַ	linsoa	to travel

Take a moment to remember: verbs in the feminine form end with ה in the singular and ות in the plural. In the masculine form the plural ends ים.

VERBS WITH THE ROOTS: ט.ו.ס, נ.ה.ג, נ.ס.ע

	נ.ס.ע	נ.ה.ג	ט.ו.ס
Gender	go by car	drive	fly
m/s	נוסע nose'a	נוהג noheg	טס tas
f/s	נוסעת nosa'at	נוהגת noheget	טסה tasa
m/p	נוסעים nos'im	נוהגים nohagim	טסים tasim
f/p	נוסעות nos'ot	נוהגות nohagot	טסים tasot

Practice

1 Can you find ten words which you have learned in this unit?

ש	ז	ס	ו	ב	ו	ט	ו	א	פ	ל	ב	ג	ה	נ
ש	ל	ח	י	ט	פ	מ	ב	ד	ת	ש	ר	ל	ב	ח
ה	נ	ח	ת	ד	ש	ס	י	ט	ר	כ	ד	ו	מ	ז
ש	ס	ל	ב	א	ז	מ	נ	ש	ד	ו	ג	ר	ב	ד
ס	ו	ב	מ	צ	ר	ק	ת	ב	כ	ר	נ	ה	ב	ס
ק	ע	ס	ס	י	י	ט	ק	ר	א	ט	ף	י	צ	ר

2 Complete the following sentences, using the words given.

רישיון-נהיגה לך רכבת שוב תחנה רבע קטנה

a האוטובוס יוצא מה _____ — The bus leaves the station.
b יש לי כרטיס ל _____ — I have a ticket to the train.
c אני רוצה מכונית _____ — I want a small car.
d השעה שבע ו _____ — The time is quarter past seven.
e אפשר לעזור _____? — May I help you?
f כרטיס הלוך ו _____ — A return ticket.
g יש לי _____ — I have a driving licence.

Go further

EXPRESSING TIME IN WEEKS AND MONTHS

שבוע	שָׁבוּעַ	shavua	week
בשבוע הבא	בַּשָּׁבוּעַ הַבָּא	bashavua haba	next week
חודש	חוֹדֶשׁ	chodesh	month
בחודש הבא	בַּחוֹדֶשׁ הַבָּא	bachodesh haba	next month

 # Test yourself

 05.07 **Listen to the audio and see if you can understand the following phrases.**

Ani rotze (rotza) latus leanglia,
bashvua haba, beyom shlishi
beshaa sheva, lamishpacha sheli.

אני רוצה לטוס לאנגליה, בשבוע הבא, ביום
שלישי בשעה שבע, למשפחה שלי.

SELF CHECK

I CAN...
...enquire about train, bus and plane timetables and buy tickets.
...express where I want to go and how to get there.
...identify the days of the week and time of day.

Getting around

In this unit you will learn how to:
▶ *ask for and understand directions.*
▶ *describe towns and cities.*
▶ *make use of organizational phrases.*

CEFR (A1): *Can recognize familiar words and phrases regarding your concrete surroundings. Can ask for and offer assistance finding directions.*

Getting around Israel

Travelling across the small country of Israel from the *north*, צפון (**tzafon**) to the *south*, דרום (**darom**) is like a journey through a biblical landscape. On your travels you will encounter places which are mentioned in the Old Testament, such as Mount Carmel, הר הכרמל (**har-ha-carmel**), Jaffa יפו (**Yafo**) and Eilat, אילת (**Eylat**). You will also reach landmarks which are holy to Christianity, נצרות (**Natzrut**), such as Nazareth, נצרת (**Natzrat**), Sea of Galilee, כנרת (**Kineret**) and, of course, the old City of Jerusalem, ירושלים (**Yerushalayim**).

Israel is a very narrow country and your journey from the *west* מערב (**ma'arav**) to the *east*, מזרח (**mizrach**) will take no time at all. In the west is the Mediterranean Sea, הים התיכון (**Ha'yam ha'tichon**) and in the east is the Jordan Valley, ירדן (**Yarden**), the Sea of Galilee and the Dead Sea, ים המלח (**Yam ha'melach**). This is directly translated as *The Sea of Salt*.

Can you see where the word for *Christianity* נצרות comes from? Can you also find the Hebrew עברית words for *sea* and *mountain*?

Vocabulary builder

06.01 **Listen and repeat these words to help you find your way around.**

PLACES OF INTEREST

רחוב	רחוב	rechov	street
עיר	עיר	ir	city, town
בנק	בנק	bank	bank
דואר	דואר	d'oar	post office
בית	בית	bayit	house
בית-כנסת	בית כנסת	beit-kneset	synagogue
כנסיה	כנסייה	knesia	church
מסגד	מסגד	misgad	mosque
רמזור	רמזור	ramzor	traffic lights
לבקר	לבקר	levaker	to visit
מקום	מקום	rechov	place

ASKING FOR DIRECTIONS

ימין	ימין	yamin	right
ימינה	ימינה	yamina	to the right
שמאל	שמאל	smol	left
שמאלה	שמאלה	smola	to the left
פינה	פינה	pina	corner
מפה	מפה	mapa	map
ליד	ליד	leyad	near
מול	מול	mul	opposite to / in front of
סליחה	סליחה	slicha	of
כאן	כאן	kan	excuse (me)
שם	שם	sham	here
קרוב	קרוב	karov	there
רח	רחוק	rachok	close (not far)

TIP

The words *synagogue* בית כנסת and *church* כנסייה share a common root כנס, which means *gathering*.

POINTS OF THE COMPASS

צפון	נ̇פון	tzafon	*north*
דרום	דרום	darom	*south*
מזרח	מזרח	mizrach	*east*
מערב	מערב	ma'rav	*west*

VERBS

The words פונה **poneh** and פונה **ponah**, respectively the male and female singular forms of *turn*, are written alike but pronounced differently. Their gender is determined by the gender of the preceding noun or name. This rule applies in other cases as well.

	turn				*go*		
m/s	פונה	פונה	pone	הולך	הולך	holech
f/s	פונה	פונה	pona	הולכת	הולכת	holechet
m/p	פונים	פונים	ponim	הולכים	הולכים	holchim
f/p	פונות	פונות	ponot	הולכות	הולכות	holchot
	visit				*go on a trip*		
m/s	מבקר	מבקר	mevaker	מטייל	מטייל	metayel
f/s	מבקרת	מבקרת	mevakeret	מטיילת	מטיילת	metayelet
m/p	מבקרים	מבקרים	mevakrim	מטיילים	מטיילים	metaylim
f/p	מבקרות	מבקרות	mevakrot	מטיילות	מטיילות	metaylot

1 **Look at the city map, and write in Hebrew what each number corresponds to. You are looking for the following:**
   supermarket school post shop synagogue corner street.
   For example, shop: 3. חנות.

2 Translate these Hebrew words into English.

a בנק

b דואר

c חנות

d ספר-בית

e כנסת-בית

f פינה

g רחוב

NEW EXPRESSIONS

?......ה איפה ,סליחה	Slicha, eifo ha...?	*Pardon, excuse me,*
?...ה	Eifo ze al hamapa?	*where is the...?*
?המפה על זה איפה	Eifo efshar lehachalif	*Where is it on the map?*
?כסף להחליף אפשר איפה	kesef?	*Where (is it possible) to*
.הספר-בית מול הדואר	Hadoar mul beit-	*change money?*
פונה את / פונה אתה	hasefer.	*The post office opposite to the*
.ימינה ברמזור	Ata pone (m/s) / at	*school.*
	pona (f) baramzor	*You turn (m/f) to the right at*
	yamina.	*the traffic lights.*
.הצהוב הבית ליד הבנק	Habank leyad habayit	*The bank near the yellow*
	hatzahov.	*house.*

PREFIXES AND SUFFIXES

The in Hebrew, when attached to a two-word noun, appears before the second word: *the school*, ספר הסבית **beit-hasefer**.

The letter ה, attached as an ending letter to names of places or directions (*left, north*), indicates the phrase: *go to. Left:* שמאל, *go to the left:* שמאלה.

The letter ב attached to a word means *at the, in* or *on:* ב. *At the corner*, בפינה **bapina**; *in the shop*, בחנות **bachanut**; *on the map*, במפה **bamapa**.

Conversation and comprehension 1

06.02 *Tom is a tourist who is visiting and driving round Tel-Aviv for the first time. Listen to the dialogue.*

a. Should Tom turn to the left at the traffic lights?

Tom	Slichah, eyfo ha muzeon?	סליחה, איפה המוזיאון?
Passenger	Ze loh rachok, leyad hapark.	זה לא רחוק, ליד הפארק.
Tom	Eifo hapark?	איפה הפארק?
Passenger	Hapark mul habank.	הפארק מול הבנק.
Tom	Be'eizeh rachov?	באיזה רחוב?
Passenger	Atah Poneh yeminah ba ramzor.	אתה פונה ימינה ברמזור.
	Zeh rachov Spinoza.	זה ברחוב שפינוזה.
Tom	Todah.	תודה.
Passenger	Be'vakasha.	בבקשה.

1 **Are the following statements true or false?**
   a The passenger knows what street the museum is on.
   b The museum is far from the park.
   c The park is opposite to the bank.

2 **Match the words to their antonyms.**

   a צפון **tzafon**   1 שם sham
   b כאן **kan**   2 מזרח mizrach
   c שמאל **smol**   3 דרום darom
   d קרוב **karov**   4 ימין yamin
   e מערב ma'**arav**   5 רחוק rachok

3 **Can you find the expressions in the conversation between Tom and the passenger which mean the following...**
   a It is not far.
   b Where is the...?
   c It is near the...
   d It is opposite to...

Language discovery

You have already learned that the word של means *to belong to* e.g. *The house of Tom* תום של הבית הבית של תום (**habayit shel Tom**).

THE DEFINITE ARTICLE

The prefix ה marks the noun as definite: *the park*, ה‎+פארק **ha park**.

You always follow the descriptive word with a ה. The exception is ב **beh** *in*, which contracts to ב **ba** when described in the definite form.

ב **be** + ה **ha** = ב **ba**

Preposition (indefinite)			Preposition (Definite)		
ליד	leyad	near	ליד (ה)	leyad	near (the)
מול	mul	opposite	מול (ה)	mul	opposite (the)
ב	be	in, at	ב	ba	in (the)

> **TIP**
>
> In Hebrew the prefix precedes the noun as well as the adjective. This differs from English. *The big park* הגדול הפארק **hapark hagadol**.

1 **Translate these phrases into English.**
   a יפה מוזיאון (muzeon yafe)
   b המפה (hamapa)
   c הרחוב (harechov)
   d רמזור (haramzor)
   e הגדול הפארק (hapark hagadol)
   f יפה הכנסייה (haknesia hayafa)
   g הבנק (habank)

You have already learned that adding a ה makes *right* and *left* definite.

| ימין | **yamin** | *right* | ימינה | **yamina** | *to the right* |
| שמאל | **smol** | *left* | שמאלה | **smola** | *to the left* |

The same principle can be applied to the four points of the compass.

2 **Express the points of the compass in the following way:** מערבה = *to the west.*

3 **Can you express the following expressions in Hebrew, practising the use of the definite article?**
   a Near the bank
   b On the road
   c In the east
   d Turn (m/s) to the left

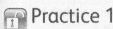

Practice 1

In this unit you have learned two important functions of the letter ה.

ה = *the* (*the* is a prefix of a noun and an adjective)

ה = indication of direction (*north*, צפון; *to the north*, צפונה)

1 **Write the Hebrew words for these places of interest.**
   a Mosque
   b School
   c Church
   d Synagogue

2 **Read the following out loud.**
   a מפה
   b רמזור
   c רחוב
   d מוזיאון יפה
   e מול בנק

3 **Translate the following into Hebrew.**
   a The map
   b The traffic light
   c On the street
   d The beautiful museum
   e Opposite the bank

Do you see the connection between these exercises?

Practice 2

1 06.03 **Listen and repeat these phrases which relate to directions.**

a קרוב
b רחוק
c תודה
d רמזור
e סליחה
f מפה
g כאן
h ליד הבנק
i להחליף כסף

2 **Translate the following phrases into English.**

a שרה פונה ימינה
b אני הולך ברחוב
c איפה אפשר להחליף כסף?
d הבנק מול הפארק
e בית הכנסת ברחוב בן-גוריון.

> **INSIGHT**
>
> Ben Gurion was the first Israeli prime minister. He read the Independence Declaration on the 14th May 1948.

3 **Fill in the missing words then read the sentence out loud.**

a Dan goes to the south — דן נוסע _____
b The big house in the corner — הבית הגדול ב _____
c Sarah and Ruth are going in the street. — רות ושרה הולכות ב _____
d Excuse me, where is the post office? — סליחה, איפה ה_____?
e It is not far, it is near the bank — זה לא _____ , זה ליד הבנק.
f When are you going to the school? — מתי _____ הולכת לבית הספר ?

4 06.04 **Listen to the following passage. When did Dan arrive in Israel?**

דן רוצה ללמוד ערבית. הוא מדבר עברית ואנגלית, ולא מבין ערבית. הוא נוסע מפריח לישראל במטוס אל-על, ב-30 בספטמבר, ביום ראשון. הוא הולך לכנסייה, ולמחיאון ישראל. ביום שני בערב דן רוצה ללכת לקונצרט עם אימא שלו.

a Where has Dan landed?
b Does Dan speak Hebrew?
c Dan likes listening to music?
d What date is Dan travelling with his mother?

Conversation and comprehension 2

06.05 *Ruth is on a plane to Israel chatting with her neighbour Tom.*
Where do Ruth's relatives live?

Tom	Lean at nosa'at?	?לאן את נוסעת
Ruth	Ani mevakeret et ha 'mispachah sheli..	.אני מבקרת את המשפחה שלי
Tom	Eifo heim garim?	?איפה הם גרים
Ruth	Ach sheli be-Yerushalim, ve shabah ve savtah sheli be Tel-Aviv.	אח שלי בירושלים, וסבא וסבתא שלי בתל-אביב.
Tom	At Nosa'at gam betiyul?	?את נוסעת גם לטייל
Ruth	Ken ani nosa'at betiyul.	.כן, אני נוסעת לטייל
Tom	Nesiyah tovah!	!נסיעה טובה
Ruth	Todah!	!תודה

06.06 *When she lands at the airport, Ruth begins chatting with a tour guide. Name three places where Ruth wants to go.*

Ruth	Ani rotzah letayel beYisrael.	.אני רוצה לטייל בישראל
Guide	Eifoh? Ba'tzafon o darom?	?איפה? בצפון או בדרום
Ruth	Batzafon vegam darom. Mekomot k'mo Natzeret, Haifa, Masada ve Eylat.	בצפון וגם בדרום. במקומות כמו נצרת, חיפה, מצדה ואילת.
Guide	Mah At rotzah la'asot?	?מה את רוצה לעשות
Ruth	Levaker mekomot historiyim, bemuzeonim, lalechet lateatron ve lekonsertim classim.	לבקר במקומות היסטוריים, במוזיאונים, ללכת לתיאטרון ולקונצרטים קלסיים.
Guide	At lo rotzah levaker beYerushalayim ve Tel-Aviv?	את לא רוצה לבקר בירושלים ובתל-אביב?
Ruth	Ken ani rotzah. Hamishpacha sheli garah be Tel-Aviv ve'Yerushalayim.	כן, אני רוצה. המשפחה שלי גרה בתל-אביב ובירושלים.
Guide	Nesiyah tovah!	!נסיעה טובה
Ruth	Thank you.	.תודה

1 Name three places that Ruth would like to visit in Israel.

2 What does Ruth want to do in Israel?

3 Where do Ruth's relatives live?

4 Tom and the tour guide wish Ruth a '_____!'

 Test yourself

Translate the following expressions into English.

1 תום פונה ימינה (tom pone yamina)

2 ?איפה הפארק היפה (eifo hapark hayafe?)

3 הבית האדום ליד בית הכנסת (beit hakneset leyad habayit haadom)

4 הבנק מול בית הספר (beit hasefer mul bank)

5 רון נוסע דרומה (ron nosea daroma)

SELF CHECK

I CAN...

●	...ask for and understand directions.
●	...describe town places and landmarks.
●	...express organizational phrases.

R2 Review units 4–6

NOUNS AND ADJECTIVES

1 Write down the adjectives that agree with the nouns. If possible, use more than one adjective for each noun.

a מכנסיים
b שמלה
c חולצות
d רחוב
e כרטיסים
f מחיאון
g מפה
h חולצה
i פארק

צהובה גדולים יקרים יפה גדול יפה (m/s) יפה (f/s) ירוק יקרה קרוב גדולה קטנה זולת

2 Do you remember that when counting, you use the feminine form? Now count the following numbers out loud in Hebrew.

a 123
b 534
c 1000
d 15
e 7
f 956
g 69
h 10
i 718
j 318
k 1948 (the date of the establishment of the state of Israel)

COLOURS

3 Match the colour to the items, making sure that the gender agrees with the noun.

a חולצה (ירוק) _____
b רמזור (צהוב) _____
c מכנסיים (אדום) _____
d שמלה (כחול) _____
e בגדים (לבן) _____
f חולצות (שחור) _____

TIME

4 Give the following times in Hebrew.

   a quarter past eight

   b half past twelve

   c 5 minutes to 11

   d 10 minutes to 4

   e 07.30

   f 18.45

   g 12.15

VERBS

5 Do you remember that most Hebrew verbs have a three letter root? Follow the example and fill in the verbs using the roots provided.

Root	נ.ס.ע	ה.ל.ך	נ.ה.ג	ר.צ.ה
m/s	נוסע			
f/s	נוסעת			
m/p	נוסעים			
f/p	נוסעות			

DIRECTIONS

6 Look at the map, decide on a place to start and give directions on how to get to the following places. Use the following words:

לדואר, לבית – הכנסת, בפינה, צריך ל..., לפנות, מול, ליד, שמאלה, ימינה

   a בית-כנסת

   b מוחיאון

   c פארק

   d פינה

   e רחוב בלפור

   f דואר

   g בית-ספר

   h חנות

   i בנק

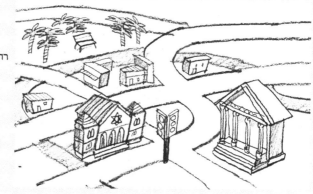

PARTICLES

7 Complete the sentences using the words provided.

a   הרכבת יוצאת _תל-אביב ומגיעה _ירושלים, בשעה 08.30

b   הבנק _____ הבית הלבן

c   איפה אפשר _החליף כסף?

d   _____ הפארק?

e   הבנק פתוח _שעה 09.00 _____ שעה 12.00

f   הבית _____ החנות

g   _____ אתה נוסע? אני נוסע בשעה 11.00.

h   הבית הזה _____ כן, הבית הזה שלי.

i   איפה אתה גר? אני גר _תל-אביב

PREFIXES AND SUFFIXES

8 Review the following then complete the exercise.

a. בית (**bayit**)	house	הבית (**habayit**)	the house
b. רחוב (**rechov**)	street	הרחוב הזה (**harechov haze**)	_____
c. בית ספר (**beyt sefer**)	school	בית הספר (**beit hasefer**)	_____
d. ימין (**yamin**)	right	ימינה (**yamina**)	_____

9 Translate the following into English.

a   אני הולך לבית הספר

b   הוא הולך ימינה

c   הבית הזה שלך?

d   כן, הבית הזה שלי

e   הבית ליד הדואר גדול

f   השמלה שלך יפה

g   החולצה האדומה, היקרה והיפה

VOCABULARY

10 Find 15 words you have learned in the grid:

ר	ד	ח			ה	ח	י	ל	ס	מ	ש		ר	ג
מ		נ		מ	ת	ו	א	ר	ת	ה	ל		מ	ד
ז	ק	נ	ב	ח			ר	ק	י	ב	ו	ט	פ	ו
ו		ו	ל	י	ה	י	ט	ב	מ	א	ס		ה	ל
ר		ת	א	ר		ו	ו	ל	מ	ס	י	ד	ג	ב

7 Israeli food

In this unit you will learn how to:
▶ *express yourself when ordering food.*
▶ *ask for items from a menu.*
▶ *describe food and drinks.*
▶ *express adjectives for food preferences.*

CEFR (A1): Can ask people for and give people things. Can get an idea of the content of menus and understand short simple descriptions, especially with visual support.

An Israeli restaurant in London

Israel is a multi-cuisine state, being a place with both the Jewish (East and West) and Arabian culinary traditions. Biblical fruits (like citruses and pomegranates), along with Eastern-Europe flavour and Yemenite herbs, are frequently served at Israeli restaurants. Everyday Arabian food, such as Humus (חומוס) and Falafel(פלאפל), have become a natural part of the Israeli diet.

Jewish Holidays are important to the Jewish Culinary heritage: Matza-balls (Passover פסח), cheese-cakes (Shavuot שבועות), Gefilte-fish (Rosh Hashana ראש השנה), among many others supply a unique flavour to the religious or national meaning of these special events.

 Did you know that in Exodus in the Bible, the land of Israel was referred to as 'אֶרֶץ זָבַת חָלָב וּדְבַשׁ' Eretz zavat chalav, u-d'vash? Can you guess what this would be in English?

Do you know the origin of this quotation: 'Land of milk and honey'?
אֶרֶץ זָבַת חָלָב וּדְבַשׁ

Vocabulary builder

 07.01 **Listen and repeat these words and phrases relating to food and drink. You will find many of these useful when in a restaurant. Can you identify any words from international cuisine?**

AT THE RESTAURANT

אוכל	אוכל	ochel	food
שתייה	שתייה	shtiya	drink (beverage)
ארוחה	ארוחה	arucha	meal
תפריט	תפריט	tafrit	menu
מסעדה	מסעדה	mis'ada	restaurant
מלצר	מלצר	meltzar	waiter
מלצרית	מלצרית	meltzarit	waitress
טיפ	טיפ	tip	tip
מלח	מלח	melach	salt
סוכר	סוכר	sukar	sugar
עוגה	עוגה	uga	cake
קפה	קפה	kafe	coffee
תה	תה	te	tea
סודה	סודה	soda	soda water
מים	מים	mayim	water
בירה	בירה	bira	beer
יין	יין	yayin	wine
חלב	חלב	chalav	milk
מרק	מרק	marak	soup
שניצל	שניצל	schnitzel	schnitzel
צ'יפס	צ'יפס	chips	chips
סלט	סלט	salat	salad
סטייק	סטייק	steak	steak
בתאבון	בתאבון!	bete'avon!	bon appétit!

USEFUL LANGUAGE

> **TIP**
> The word *cutlery*, סכו״ם **sakum** is the acronym of *spoon*, *knife* and *fork*.

שולחן	שולחן	shulchan	table
כוס	כוס	cos	glass
ספל	ספל	sefel	cup
צלחת	צלחת	tzalachat	plate
סכין	סכין	sakin	knife

 7 Israeli food   67

מזלג	מ&לג	mazleg	fork
כף	כ&ף	kaf	spoon
כפית	כפית	kapit	teaspoon

VERBS

You have already learned the verbs *want* and *ask for*. Refresh your memory before you learn how to order from a menu.

	eat		*drink*	
m/s	אוכל	**ochel**	שותה	**shote**
f/s	אוכלת	**ochelet**	שותה	**shota**
m/p	אוכלים	**ochlim**	שותים	**shotim**
f/p	אוכלות	**ochlot**	שותות	**shotot**

	want		*ask for*	
m/s	רוצה	**rotze**	מבקש	**mevakesh**
f/s	רוצה	**rotza**	מבקשת	**mevakeshet**
m/p	רוצים	**rotzim**	מבקשים	**mevakshim**
f/p	רוצות	**rotzot**	מבקשות	**mevakshot**

NEW EXPRESSIONS

07.02 Listen and repeat these new food-related expressions.

האוכל טעים?	ha'ochel taeem?	*Is the food tasty?*
טוב מאוד.	tov me'od.	*very good*
מידי מלוח/מתוק ...	Miday maluach/matok...	*Too salty/sweet...*
אפשר לקבל כוס מים?	Efshar lekabel kos mayim?	*May I have a glass of water?*
שולחן לשניים בבקשה.	Shulchan leshnayim, bevakasha.	*A table for two please.*
ארוחות – בוקר, צהריים, ערב.	Aruchat: boker, Tzaharayim, erev.	*Meal: breakfast, lunch, dinner*
מה בשבילך, בבקשה?	Ma bishvilcha (m) bishvilech (f), bevakasha?	*What would you like to have? (Lit: What for you, please?)*
הנה ה...	Hine ha...	*Here is the...*
גם	gam	*also, too*
עוד	od	*more*
רק	rak	*just, only*
פחות	pachot	*less*
מספיק, די	maspik, day (sounds like die)	*enough*

68

Conversation and comprehension 1

07.03 *Dan and Rose meet at their favourite spot in Dizengoff Square. The waiter approaches them for their order.*

1 Can you identify what kind of restaurant this is?

Waiter	Shulchan leshnayim?	?שולחן לשניים
Dan	Ken, toda.	.כן, תודה
Waiter	Hine ha'tafrit.	.הנה התפריט
Dan & Rose	Toda.	.תודה
Dan	Ani mevakesh sefel café veuga.	.אני מבקש ספל קפה ועוגה
Waiter	Od mashehu?	?עוד משהו
Dan	Lo, toda.	.לא תודה
Waiter to Rose	Ma bishvilech, bevakash?	?מה בשבילך, בבקשה
Rose	Sefel kafe, bevakash.	.ספל קפה, בבקשה
Waiter	Gam uga?	?גם עוגה
Rose	Lo toda, rak kafe vekos mayim.	.לא תודה, רק קפה וכוס מים
Waiter	Bevakasha.	.בבקשה

2 Are the following statements true or false?
   a Rose asks for a cup of coffee.
   b Dan asks for a glass of water.
   c Rose is having a slice of cake.
   d Dan will have a cup of coffee and some cake.
   e The waiter hands them the menu.

 3 Find the true statements you have identified within the conversation. Now see if you can repeat these conversation lines in Hebrew without looking at the conversation.

Language discovery

1 Match the Hebrew and English phrases.
   a Something else.   **1** .רק קפה
   b Also a piece of cake.   **2** .עוד משהו
   c Just coffee.   **3** .גם עוגה

MORE THAN AND LESS THAN

פחות **means** *less*

...פחות מ **means** *less than...*

יותר **means** *more*

...יותר מ **means** *more than...*

As you can see there are more words and variations of the expression *more than / less than* in Hebrew than there are in English. In Hebrew there is no difference between *much* and *many*.

2 Read through the short passage and fill in the missing words using the words listed.

דַי מספיק; זה מספיק; עוד רק קצת פחות רק

Ben visits the Green family at their home and coffee is served. Mrs Green pours the coffee. 'Would you like to have some milk?' '(*Just a little*) _____', Ben says. Mrs. Green pours the milk and Ben gestures for her to stop. '(*That's enough*) _____'. 'How much sugar?' '(*Just*) _____ one teaspoon.' 'Would you like to have some cake?' 'Yes, thank you.' Mrs Green cuts a piece of cake and asks if that much is OK? 'No', says Ben, '(*less*) _____'. As often is the case in Israel, they talk about politics and start arguing. '(*Enough with*) _____ politics', says Mrs Green, 'do you want some (*more*) _____ cake?'

3 07.04 **Listen to these questions which you may be asked when being served food. Can you provide answers to these questions?**

a ?האוכל טעים

b אפשר לקבל כוס מים?

c אתם רוצים שולחן לשניים?

d אתה רוצה פחות סלט?

4 What are these people saying? Read and translate the following sentences.

a האוכל טעים מאוד _____

b אני אוכלת סטייק צ'יפס _____

c כוס בירה, בבקשה _____

d יש אוכל טוב בתפריט _____

e האוכל מלוח מידי _____

Listen and understand

Listen to the following passage.

a Is falafel exclusively of Israeli origin?

בישראל אוכלים פלאפל וסלט בפיתה – זה אוכל
אורייניטאלי, לא ישראלי אורגינאלי. בישראל אוכלים גם
שניצל בפיתה, ושותים קוקה-קולה. באמריקה אוכלים
המבורגר מגרמניה וצ'יפס מצרפת (France).

b What is the origin of the hamburger?

c Which food is Middle Eastern?

d Which foods go with pita bread?

e Do Israelis eat salad?

 Conversation and comprehension 2

Tom and Rachel celebrate their wedding anniversary in a restaurant. The waiter leads them to their table and hands them the menus.

1 What does Rachel order?

Tom	Ma at rotza le'echol?	מה את רוצה לאכול?
Rachel	Ani rotza steak vesalat.	אני רוצה סטייק וסלט.
Tom	At shota yayin?	את שותה יין?
Rachel	Ken, yayin adom.	כן, יין אדום.
Waiter	Ma atem rotzim?	מה אתם מבקשים?
Tom	La steak, salat veyayin adom.	לה סטייק, סלט ויין אדום.
Waiter	Eich at rotza et hasteak?	איך את רוצה את הסטייק?
Rachel	'Medium well' bevakasha.	**'Medium-well'** בבקשה.
Waiter	Ma lecha?	מה לך?
Tom	Li schnitzel, chips, vekos yayin lavan, bevakasha.	לי שניצל, צ'יפס, וכוס יין לבן, בבקשה.

2 Answer these questions about the conversation.

a Who drinks white wine?

b Does Rachel like her steak medium rare?

c Who drinks water?

d Can you find the Hebrew for *for her* and *for me*.

Can you see the connection between לבקש, *to ask* **and** בבקשה, *please*?

FOR ME, FOR YOU

לי	*לִי*	li	*for me*
לך	*לְךָ*	lecha	*for you (m/s)*
לך	*לָךְ*	lach	*for you (f/s)*
לו	*לוֹ*	lo	*for him*
לה	*לָהּ*	la	*for her*
לנו	*לָנוּ*	lanu	*for us*
לכם	*לָכֶם*	lachem	*for you (m/p)*
לכן	*לָכֶן*	lichen	*for you (f/p)*
להם	*לָהֶם*	lahem	*for them (m/p)*
להן	*לָהֶן*	lahen	*for them (f/p)*

2 Translate the underlined words.

 a ‏<u>לי</u> רק מים בבקשה

 b אני לא רוצה <u>הרבה</u> סלט

 c כוס בירה <u>לו ולה</u>

 d אני <u>מבקש</u> תפריט, <u>לה וגם ל</u>

3 In this unit you have learned the phrases *for me* לי **li** and *for you*, לך **lach / lechah**. In Unit 2, the words *my*, שלי and *your*, שלך were introduced. Read to the questions then use these determiners to answer in Hebrew.

a   של מי הבית הזה?

b   הגיטרה הזו שלך?

c   יש לה אוטו

d   לך, קפה או תה?

e   הבגד הזה שלו

4 Read through the menu below. Answer the questions then write down what would you like to eat.

מנות ראשונות	מנה עיקרית	מנות אחרונות	משקאות
Starters	Main course	deserts	drinks
סלט	סטייק	קפה, תה	יין
פלפל	שניצל	עוגה	מים
חומוס(humus)	צ׳יפס	סלט פירות	בירה
		(salat peyrot)	סודה

1   אני _____ מה אתה רוצה לאכול?

2   אני _____ מה את רוצה לאכול?

3   אני _____ מה אתה רוצה לשתות?

4   אני _____ מה את רוצה לשתות?

Go further

POSSESSIVE PRONOUNS

	I	אני	**ani**	for me	לי	**li**	mine	שלי	**sheli**
m/s	you	אתה	**ata**	for you	לך	**lecha**	your	שלך	**shelcha**
f/s	you	את	**at**	for you	לך	**lach**	your	שלך	**shelach**
m/s	he	הוא	**hoo**	for him	לו	**lo**	his	שלו	**shelo**
f/s	she	היא	**hee**	for her	לה	**la**	hers	שלה	**shela**
	we	אנחנו	**anachnu**	for us	לנו	**lanu**	our	שלנו	**shelanu**
m/p	you	אתם	**atem**	for you	לכם	**lachem**	your	שלכם	**shelachem**
f/p	you	אתן	**aten**	for you	לכן	**lachen**	your	שלכן	**shelachn**
m/p	they	הם	**hem**	for them	להם	**lahem**	their	שלהם	**shelahem**
f/p	they	הן	**hen**	for them	להן	**lahen**	their	שלהן	**shelahen**

 Do you notice the connection between the possessive pronouns and the corresponding personal pronouns?

SELF CHECK

I CAN...

⬤	. . . order food from a menu.
⬤	. . . ask for and receive things.
⬤	. . . name types of food and drinks and describe preferences.
⬤	. . . express adjectives for food.

8 Daily life

In this unit you will learn how to:
▶ *discuss daily activities and habits.*
▶ *review and express time.*
▶ *describe your home and environment.*
▶ *read and understand a list of rules.*

CEFR (A1): Can describe yourself, your concrete surroundings and where you live. Can discuss personal details, habits and professions using verbs in the singular, plural, feminine and masculine forms.

Working in Israel

How could you describe the early Israeli pioneers? In 1916, before Israel's independence, Joseph Trumpeldor יוֹסֵף טרוּמְפֶּלְדּוֹר, an early pioneering hero gave us a prolific answer to this question.

'What are the needs of the "national mechanism"? If it is a wheel – I am it, and if a nail or a screw or a fly-wheel – take me. I am a digger, a soldier, a doctor, a lawyer, a teacher, a water-drawer. I do all. I have no face, no psychology, no feelings, I even have no name. I am the pure ideology of service. I obey just to one command: "to build."'

The early Israeli pioneers חלוצים *chalutzim* faced the challenge of irrigating and developing the mostly uninhabitable farmland. A great deal has changed since the early 1900s. Today, Israel is a modern country, known for its developed agriculture חקלאות, medical רפואה and High-Tech מחשבים innovations. The renewal of the Hebrew language includes new names for professions, based on ancient words. For example, computer, מחשב (machshev) originates from the word thought, מחשבה (machshava).

Can you guess which professions originate from these words?

נהג איבנק

Vocabulary builder

 08.01 **Listen and repeat these words and phrases relating to work, daily routine, and from around the home.**

WORK AND PROFESSIONS

עבודה	עבודה	avoda	work (noun)
לעבוד	לעבוד	la'avod	to work (gerund)
כול יום	כול יום	kol·yom	every day
היי-טק	היי–טק	high-tech	high-tech
יום-עבודה	יום–עבודה	yom-avoda	workday

DAILY ROUTINE

מאוחר	מאוחר	meuchar	late
מוקדם	מוקדם	mukdam	early
רוצה להיות	רוצה להיות	rotze liheyot (m)	wants to be
רוצה להיות	רוצה להיות	rotza liheyot (f)	wants to be
סוף	סוף	sof	end
שבוע	שבוע	shavua	week
ארוחת-בוקר	ארוחת–בוקר	aruchat-boker	breakfast
ארוחת ערב	ארוחת ערב	aruchat-erev	supper

AROUND THE HOME

מטבח	מטבח	mitbach	kitchen
חדר אוכל	חדר אוכל	chadar ochel	dining room
חדר אורחים	חדר אורחים	chadar orchim	lounge
חדר שינה	חדר שינה	chadar sheyna	bedroom

> **LITERAL TRANSLATIONS**
>
> סוף שבוע (end + week) describes the weekend.
> Bedroom חדר שינה in Hebrew is translated literally as sleeping room in English.

Can you see the connection between the verbs *to sleep* and *to eat*, and the rooms where these activities take place: *the dining room* and *bedroom?* לישון – חדר שינה ; חדר אוכל – לאכול

You can already use the new vocabulary to create new sentences. Now match the phrases with their missing words.

a	ב- 09.00 _____ יום עבודה	1	ארוחת ערב
b	הסטודנט לומד ב _____	2	לישון
c	אני הולך _____ בשעה 23.00	3	אוניברסיטה
d	הסטודנט רוצה להיות _____	4	מתחיל
e	אנחנו אוכלים _____ בשעה 19.00	5	דוקטור
f	אני אוכל בבוקר _____	6	אוכלים
g	אנחנו _____ בחדר האוכל	7	טלביזיה
h	אנחנו רואים _____ בחדר האורחים	8	ארוחת-בוקר

NEW EXPRESSIONS

כל יום– אותו דבר.	Kol yom – oto davar.	*Every day – the same.*
מהר, מהר, אני מאחר.	Maher, maher, ani me'acher.	*Quickly, quickly, I am late.*
מוקדם בבוקר.	Mukdam baboker.	*Early in the morning.*
מאוחר בלילה.	Meuchar balayla.	*Late at night.*
יותר מוקדם בבוקר.	Yoter mukdam baboker.	*Earlier in the morning.*
יותר מאוחר בלילה.	Yoter meuchar balayla.	*Later at night.*
אני אוהב לקרוא ספר, לראות טלביזיה, לשמוע רדיו, לשמוע מוסיקה.	Ani ohev likro sefer, lir'ot televizia, lishmoa radio, lishmoa musika.	*I like (love) to read a book, to watch TV, to listen to the radio, to listen to music.*
רק בסוף השבוע.	Rak besof hashavua.	*Only at the weekend.*

VERBS

	to begin להתחיל **lehatchil**		*to be late* לאחר **leacher**		*to get up* לקום **lakum**	
m/s	מתחיל	matchil	מאחר	me'acher	קם	kam
f/s	מתחילה	matchila	מאחרת	meacheret	קמה	kama
m/p	מתחילים	matchilim	מאחרים	meacharim	קמים	kamim
f/p	מתחילות	matchilot	מאחרות	meacharot	קמות	kamot

78

	to love			to sleep			to read	
	לאהוב			לישון			לקרוא	
	le'ehov			**lishon**			**likroh**	
m/s	אוהב	**ohev**	ישן	**yashen**	קורא	**kore**
f/s	אוהבת	**ohevet**	ישנה	**yeshena**	קוראת	**koret**
m/p	אוהבים	**ohavim**	ישנים	**yeshenim**	קוראים	**kor'im**
f/p	אוהבות	**ohavot**	ישנות	**yeshenot**	קוראות	**kor'ot**

Take a moment to remember: You have already learned the endings of verbs in their feminine and masculine, singular and plural, forms (see above), and that the Hebrew gerund (*to begin*, etc.) starts with ל (*l*).

Conversation and comprehension 1

08.02 *Dan sits down with his mother and father for a meal. At what time of day are they eating?*

Mother	Boker tov.	בוקר טוב.
Family	Boker tov.	בוקר טוב.
Mother	Aba, ma ata rotze le'echol?	אבא, מה אתה רוצה לאכול?
Father	Rak kafe, bevakasha.	רק קפה, בבקשה.
Mother	Dan, ata rotze popcorn bechalav?	דן, אתה רוצה פופקורן בחלב?
Dan	Lo, toda, ani memaher launiversita.	לא, תודה, אני ממהר לאוניברסיטה.
Mother	Kol yom oto davar. Ata tzarich lakum yoter mukdam.	כל יום אותו דבר. אתה צריך לקום יותר מוקדם.

1 Answer these questions.

  a Who eats a sandwich?
  b Does Dan usually get up early in the morning?
  c Who studies at university?
  d What is Dan doing every morning?

2 Now match the English and Hebrew words.

  a good **morning**   **1** אותו דבר
  b just **coffee**   **2** רק קפה
  c the **same**   **3** מוקדם
  d **early**   **4** בוקר טוב
  e I am in a **hurry**   **5** אני ממהר

Language discovery

The masculine and feminine, singular and plural endings of verbs have common characteristics.

The masculine and feminine, singular and plural endings of nouns share these common characteristics.

Read through the last conversation again, and think about how the different inflections you have learned apply to the verbs and nouns which were introduced to you in the conversation held between Dan and his family.

VERBS

Knowing the rules of the inflection of verbs and nouns is very helpful. The endings indicate the gender, and whether the word is singular or plural.

m/s	אוכל	ochel	ממהר	memaher
f/s	אוכלת	ochelet	ממהרת	memaheret
m/p	אוכלים	ochlim	ממהרים	memaharim
f/p	אוכלות	ochlot	ממהרות	memaharot
m/s	קם	kam	רוצה	rotze
f/s	קמה	kama	רוצה	rotza
m/p	קמים מים	kamim	רוצים	rotzim
f/p	קמות	kamot	רוצות	rotzot

NOUNS

m/s	סטודנט	student	אומן	oman		
f/s	סטודנטית	studentit	אומנית	omanit	עבודה	avoda
m/p	סטודנטים	studentim	אומנים	omanim		
f/p	סטודנטיות	studentiyot	אומניות	omaniyot	עבודות	avodot
m/s	[----]	[----]	יום	yom	רופא	
f/s	עבודה	avoda	[----]	[----]	רופאה	
m/p	[----]	[----]	ימים	yamim	רופאים	
f/p	עבודות	avodot	[----]	[----]	רופאות	
m/s	רופא	rofe				
f/s	רופאה	rof'a				
m/p	רופאים	rof'im				
f/p	רופאות	rof'ot				

1 **Identify whether the following are singular or plural, masculine or feminine. The first one in each section has been done for you.**

PROFESSIONS

a שוטרים m/p

b רופאות

c סטודנט

d חקלאיות

e מורים

f מלצר

NOUNS

g עבודה f/s

h שעה

i אומניות

j ארוחה

k ימים

l רמזור

m כוסות

n צלחות

 2 **By following the example below, read the questions out loud and give your own answers in Hebrew. Note: stay true to the gender.**

Q:	את קמה מוקדם בבוקר?	**Q:**	At kama mukdam baboker?
A:	כן, אני קמה מוקדם בבוקר	**A:**	Ken, ani kama mukdam baboker / lo, ani lo kama mukdam baboke.
	לא, אני לא קמה מוקדם בבוקה.		
Q:	אתה הולך לעבודה כל יום?		Ata holech kol yom la'avoda?
Q:	אתה אוכל ארוחת בוקר?		Ata ochel aruchat boker?
Q:	את שותה קפה בבוקר?		At shota kafe baboker?

 Listen and understand

08.03 **Listen to the following text.**

a. Who gets up early in the morning?

רות נוסעת כל יום לעבודה. היא קמה מוקדם, אוכלת ארוחת בוקר ושותה קפה. בצהריים היא אוכלת בעבודה. גם רון נוסע לעבודה. הוא קם מאוחר, לא אוכל ארוחת בוקר ורק שותה קפה. בצהריים הוא אוכל באוניברסיטה.

b Does Ron eat breakfast?

c Where does Ruth eat her lunch?

d Do Ron and Ruth drink coffee?

e Where is Ron having his lunch?

Conversation and comprehension 2

08.04 *Tom and Rachel are discussing their daily routine. Follow the conversation and answer the questions.*

1 Who is able to start work at 9 o'clock?

Rachel	Anachnu ochlim aruchat erev Besha'a sheva, bachadar haochel shelanu. Ba'erev ani ro'aa televisia bachadar haorchim, shoma'at radio, o koret sefer bachadar hasheyna. Ani holechet lishon mukdam, ki ani tzricha lakum mukdam Baboker.	אנחנו אוכלים ארוחת ערב בשעה שבע, בחדר האוכל שלנו. בערב אני רואה טלביזיה בחדר האורחים, שומעת רדיו או קוראת ספר בחדר השינה. אני הולכת לישון מוקדם, כי אני צריכה לקום מוקדם בבוקר.
Tom	Anachnu ochlim aruchat erev be'shmone bamitbach Shelanu. Anachnu ochlim bachadar ha'ochel rak pa'am beshavu'a, besof hashavua. Baerev ani shome'a musika, o ro'e televizia bachadar haorchim sheli. Ani lo ohev likro sfarim. Ani holech lishon meuchar balayla, veani lo ohev lakum mukdam baboker.	אנחנו אוכלים ארוחת ערב בשמונה במטבח שלנו. אנחנו אוכלים בחדר האוכל רק פעם בשבוע, בסוף השבוע. בערב אני שומע מוסיקה, או רואה טלביזיה בחדר האורחים. אני לא אוהב לקרוא ספרים. אני הולך לישון מאוחר בלילה, ואני לא אוהב לקום מוקדם בבוקר.

2 Answer the following questions.

a Who should start work later than 9 o'clock?

b When do Rachel and Tom have their dinner?

c Do they read books?

d Where do they eat their dinner?

e Where stands Rachel's television, and where is Tom's TV?

Go back and read the conversation between Tom and Rachel, and see if you can describe your own daily routine in Hebrew.

2 Match the Hebrew with the English translations.

a Study	**1** אמבטיה		
b Bathroom	**2** מטבח		
c Dining room	**3** חדר שינה		
d Kitchen	**4** חדר אורחים		
e Bedroom	**5** חדר אוכל		
f Guest room	**6** חדר עבודה		

The word for *study* in Hebrew is *workroom* חדר עבודה. Remembering that most Hebrew words have a three-letter root can help you match new words to those you may know already.

3 Match the gerund to the verb.

Gerund		Verb	
a להתחיל	lehatchil	*to begin*	**1** עובד
b לעבוד	laavod	*to work*	**2** ישן
c לישון	lishon	*to sleep*	**3** מתחיל
d לאכול	le'**echol**	*to eat*	**4** מאחר
e לאחר	**leacher**	*to be late*	**5** אוכל

Go further

SLANG EXPRESSIONS

English	literal translation	Hebrew	
hard working	*works like a donkey*	עובד כמו חמור	**oved kemo chamor**
makes a pass at her	*starts with her*	מתחיל איתה	**matchil ita**
all is well that ends well	*(if the) end is well everything is well*	סוף טוב הכל טוב	**sof tov hakol tov**

?? Test yourself

1 Translate into English.

   a אתה צריך לקום מוקדם יותר

   b אני קוראת בחדר השינה

   c אבא שלי דוקטור

   d הם עובדים במטבח

   e היא רוצה להיות רפעה

2 Translate into Hebrew.

   a I get up (m) early in the morning.

   b I drink (f) coffee every morning.

   c In the evening he reads books.

   d We eat (m)in the dining room.

   e She loves to watch TV.

SELF CHECK

	I CAN. . .
○	...describe my daily routine and meals.
○	...discuss professions, work and study.
○	...talk about leisure activities in the evening.
○	...describe my home and environment.

Sports and entertainment

In this unit you will learn how to:
▶ *discuss leisure activities.*
▶ *describe activities, likes and dislikes.*
▶ *understand a short review or interview.*

CEFR *(A1): Can make introductions and answer questions about personal information and write short simple notes. Can respond to information and announcements relating to their surroundings.*

National Theatre of Israel

The National Theatre תיאטרון of Israel is called Habima, 'The Stage'. Located in Habima square in Tel-Aviv, it was one of the first Hebrew speaking theatres with a permanent repertoire. The theatre troupe was originally founded in Poland in 1912 as a traditional Yiddish יידיש Theatre which put on productions based around Jewish themes. In 1918 it began operating from Moscow מוסקבה, under the auspices of the Moscow Art Theatre. This is considered the real beginning of the theatre.

In 1926, the theatre went on tour. While in New York some of the troupe decided to stay in America while others returned to settle in British Mandate Palestine פלשתינה. And it is here that Habima has remained as a national Jewish theatre to the present day, where it has received many plaudits and acclaim on the world stage.

> **TIP**
> Where does the name Palestine come from? The Philistine people invaded the land in the 12th century BC, around a hundred years after the Israelites.

 Which Hebrew word originates from the Greek word thea (*show* or *vision*)?

Vocabulary builder

 09.01 Listen and repeat the following words and phrases relating to sport. How many international words can you recognize?

SPORT

ספורט	‏ספורט	sport	sport
כדורגל	‏כדורגל	kaduregel	football
טניס	‏טניס	tennis	tennis
ג׳ודו	‏ג׳ודו	judo	judo
חדר כושר	‏חדר כושר	chadar kosher	gym
אולימפיאדה	‏אולימפיאדה	olympiada	olympiad
פעם בשבוע	‏פעם בשבוע	pa'am b'shavua	once a week

ART AND CULTURE

 09.02 Listen and repeat the following words and phrases relating to arts and culture.

קולנוע	‏קולנוע	kolnoa	cinema
תיאטרון	‏תיאטרון	teatron	theatre
סרט	‏סרט	seret	film
הצגה	‏הצגה	hatzaga	show
מוסיקה קלאסית	‏מוסיקה קלאסית	musika klassit	classical music
כרטיס	‏כרטיס	kartis	ticket
קופה	‏קופה	kupa	box office
פתוח	‏פתוח	patuach	open
סגור	‏סגור	sagur	closed
אינטרנט	‏אינטרנט	internet	internet
לגלוש	‏לגלוש	liglosh	to surf
מהר	‏מהר	maher	quickly
לאט	‏לאט	le'at	slowly
מעניין	‏מעניין	meanyen	interesting
אוהב	‏אוהב	ohev	like
לא אוהב	‏לא אוהב	lo ohev	don't like
ריצה	‏ריצה	ritza	running

 TIP
The adjective follows the gender of the noun, for example *good film* סרט טוב (m), *good show* הצגה טובה (f), *very good film* סרט טוב מאוד (m).

The word כדורגל is a combined word כדור + רגל (foot + ball). Can you work out the Hebrew for basket + סל ball?

VERBS RELATING TO SPORT

	to run לרוץ			*to swim* לשחות	
m/s	רץ	**ratz**		שוחה	**soche**
f/s	רצה	**ratza**		שוחה	**socha**
m/p	רצים	**ratzim**		שוחים	**sochim**
f/p	רצות	**ratzot**		שוחות	**sochot**

	to surf לגלוש			*to read* לקרוא	
m/s	גולש	**golesh**		קורא	**kore**
f/s	גולשת	**goleshet**		קוראת	**koret**
m/p	גולשים	**golshim**		קוראים	**kor'im**
f/p	גולשות	**golshot**		קוראות	**kor'ot**

	to go ללכת			*to act (play)* לשחק	
m/s	הולך	**holech**		משחק	**mesachek**
f/s	הולכת	**holechet**		משחקת	**mesacheket**
m/p	הולכים	**holchim**		משחקים	**mesachkim**
f/p	הולכות	**holchot**		משחקות	**mesachakot**

> **REMEMBER**
>
> 1 The translation of the words *actor* and *actress* in Hebrew is *player* שחקן. This term can also used in games like football and basketball.
> 2 Remember that in Hebrew the adjective follows the noun. The word for a 'hit' film or play in Hebrew is the same as in English – להיט **lahit**.

NEW EXPRESSIONS

אני הולך לקונצרט, לסרט, להצגה.	Ani holech lekontzert, leseret, lehatzaga.	I go to a concert, a film, a theatre show.
מוסיקה קלאסית, ג'אז.	musica classit, jazz	classical music, jazz
הסרט הזה להיט.	Haseret haze lahit.	This film is a hit.
הצגה טובה מאוד /	hatzaga tova meod /	a very good show / film
סרט טוב מאוד.	seret tov meod	

| שחקן טוב / שחקנית טובה. | sachkan tov / sachkanit tova | a good actor / a good actress |
| הוא שוחה מהר / היא רצה מהר. | hoo soche maher / hee ratza maher | he swims quickly / she runs quickly (adverb) |

TIP

The letter ג with an apostrophe ג׳ sounds like a combination of the letters j and g as in the examples judo ג׳ודו and jazz ג׳אז.

Conversation and comprehension 1

09.03 *David and Rose meet at a coffee shop and start talking about films and the theatre. Listen to their conversation. Do you think David and Rose going out together this evening?*

Rose	Ani holechet laseret 'Harry Potter'. Ze seret tov. Maggie Smith sachkanit tova meod.	אני הולכת לסרט 'הארי פוטר', זה סרט טוב. מגי סמית' שחקנית טובה מאוד.
David	Ani lo ohev et hakolnoa. Ani ohev teatron vecontzertim klaseim.	אני לא אוהב את הקולנוע. אני אוהב תיאטרון וקונצרטים קלאסיים.
Rose	Yesh hatzaga tova bateatron?	יש הצגה טובה בתיאטרון?
David	Ken hamachaze Cabaret, hamusika tova me'od.	כן, המחזה קברט, המוסיקה טובה מאוד.
Rose	Yesh lecha kartisim?	יש לך כרטיסים?
David	Ken, yesh li kartisim. Yes lach kartisim?	כן, יש לי. יש לך כרטיסים?
Rose	Ke, yesh li. Ani holechet haerev.	כן, יש לי. אני הולכת הערב.

1 **Listen to the conversation and answer these questions.**

   a Which play is on the stage in the theatre?

   b Who is going to the cinema?

   c Who has tickets?

   d Who is going out this evening?

 # Language discovery

 TIP

To a question that requires a positive or a negative answer, you can start with the word *yes* כן or *no* לא, and use the question again in your answer.

1 **Match these English words and names with the Hebrew translations.**

a Maggie Smith	**1**	לא אוהב קולנוע
b David	**2**	מחזה מוסיקאלי
c cabaret	**3**	אוהבת קולנוע
d music	**4**	שחקנית
e Rose	**5**	קלאסית

ADJECTIVES AND ADVERBS

The adjective follows the noun and should match the gender of the noun. Similarly, adverbs always follow the verb.

2 **Match the opposites.**

6. אין   5. אוהב   4. טוב   3. מהר   1. בכושר

E. רע   D. יש   C. לא בכושר   B. לא אוהב   A. לאט

3 **Match the adverbs to the verbs.**

a מהר (maher)	**1**	רצה (ratza)
b לאט (leat)	**2**	שוחה (socha)
c טוב (tov)	**3**	משחק (mesachek)
d רע (ra)	**4**	הולכת (holechet)

4 **Match the adjectives to the nouns. There is sometimes more than one option.**

a טוב (tov)	**1**	שחקן (sachkan)
b טובה (tova)	**2**	סרט (seret)
c מאוד טוב (tov meod)	**3**	הצגה (hatzaga)
d יפה (yafe)	**4**	שחקנית
e מעניין (meanyen)	**5**	ספר

5 **Give the gender of these verbs and say whether they are plural or singular.**

a הולכת

b אוהב

c טובה

d קוראים

e אוהבות

f הצגות

g טובים

h קוראת

 6 09.04 **You are an attendant in the box office of a theatre and are approached by a customer. Listen to the customer and answer his questions.**

You	Shalom, ken bevakash?	שלום, כן בבקשה?
Customer	Yesh kartisim lahatzaga?	יש כרטיסים להצגה?
You	Ken, yesh.	כן, יש.
Customer	Yesh kartisim leyom shlishi?	יש כרטיסים ליום שלישי?
You	Lo, rak leyom reviee.	לא, רק ליום רביעי.
Customer	Tov. Ani mevakesh shney kartisim. leyom reviee	טוב, אני מבקש שני כרטיסים ליום רביעי
You	Bevakasha, shney kartisim leyom reviee.	בבקשה, שני כרטיסים ליום רביעי.
Customer	Toda.	תודה.
You	_____ Toda, veshalom.	_____ תודה ושלום.

 # Listen and understand

09.05 **Listen to this interview with the actress, Mrs. Maron.**

1 Does she like to go to the opera?

| Ani sachkanit teatron, bat 35. Ani ohevet lir'ot sratim, balet velishmoa musikat jazz. Opera ani lo ohevet.

Pa'amayim beshavua ani holechet lachadar kosher, veani gam socha veratza bapark. | אני שחקנית תיאטרון, בת 35. אני אוהבת לראות סרטים, בלט ולשמוע מוסיקת ג'אז. אופרה אני לא אוהבת.

פעמיים בשבוע אני הולכת לחדר כושר, ואני גם שוחה ורצה בפארק. |

2 **Are the following statements about Mrs Maron true or false?**
   a She likes to swim.
   b She dislikes to go to the gym.
   c She runs 35 minutes every day.
   d She likes to watch films.

3 **Fill in the calling card for Mrs Maron.**

Profession: _____
Age: _____
Three artistic preferences: _____
Dislikes: _____
Sporting activities: _____

 Conversation and comprehension 2

09.06 *Mark, an Olympic swimmer, is being interviewed by a journalist. Can you guess what the word* מדליה **medalia** *means?*

Q	Ata rak soche?	?אתה רק שוחה
A	Lo, ani ratz gam.	.לא, אני רץ גם
Q	Ata gam mesachek kaduregel o kadursal?	?אתה גם משחק, כדורגל או כדורסל
A	Lo, ani ohev lesachek, aval ein li zman.	.לא, אני אוהב לשחק, אבל אין לי זמן
Q	Kama peamim beshavua ata soche?	?כמה פעמים בשבוע אתה שוחה
A	Ani soche kol yom.	.אני שוחה כל יום
Q	Kama shaot beyom ata	?כמה שעות ביום אתה שוחה
A	Sheatayim o shalosh kol yom.	.שעתיים או שלוש כל יום
Q	Ata rotze lekabel medalia?	?אתה רוצה לקבל מדליה
A	Ani meod rotze.	.אני מאוד רוצה

1 **Answer these questions.**
   a How many hours per day does the swimmer practise?
   b Will he get a medal in the Olympic Games?
   c Is his only sport swimming?

2 **Review the vocabulary. Which of these words and phrases relate to sport and which to the arts?**

a	באלט	ballet
b	אופרה	opera
c	חדר כושר	chadar kosher
d	מוסיקה קלאסית	musika classit
e	ג'אז	jazz
f	אולימפיאדה	olympiada
g	כדורגל	kaduregal
h	ריצה	ritza
i	תיאטרון	teatron
j	שחייה	shechiah
k	כדורסל	kadursal

3 09.06 **Listen to the questions and give a positive and negative reply. The first question has been done for you.**

a Q: ‏?הוא רץ מהר A: ‏כן, הוא רץ מהר. ‏לא, הוא לא רץ מהר

b ‏יש לך כרטיס?

c ‏הוא שחקן טוב?

d ‏הקופה פתוחה?

e ‏אתה אוהב מוסיקת ג'אז?

4 **Read the announcements.**

הערב – סרט בסינמטק	חדר הכושר פתוח:	הקופה פתוחה
cinematic	מ 07.00 – עד 20.00 –	
אין כרטיסים – הקופה סגורה	הצגה חדשה בתיאטרון "הבימה"	פיגארו באופרה

5 **David writes the following profile for himself on a dating site.**

‏אני בן 25, אני סטודנט, אני אוהב ספורט; משחק כדורגל ורץ. אני גם אוהב ללכת לקולנוע, לשמוע מוסיקה ולקרוא ספרים.

Rachel presents herself on the same site. Her age and interests are similar to his. Write them down, using the following words to help you:

‏אני בת רצה, משחקת, אוהבת, סטודנטית

Go further

Enrich your vocabulary with these additional useful words.

(פרמיירה) הצגת בכורה	**premiera** **(hatzagat bchora)**	*premiere*
בלרינה	**ballerina**	*ballerina*
קומדיה	**comedia**	*comedy*
טרגדיה	**tragedia**	*tragedy*
תזמורת	**tizmoret**	*orchestra*
מנצח	**menatzeach** (also **winner**)	*conductor*
במה	**bama**	*stage*
שופט	**shofet** (also **judge**)	*referee*
בריכת שחייה	**breychat schiya**	*swimming pool*
בריכה	**breycha**	*pool*

SELF CHECK

I CAN...

○ . . . discuss leisure activities relating to sport and the arts.

○ . . . express my likes and dislikes.

○ . . . use adverbs and adjectives correctly.

○ . . . write a short description of myself.

○ . . . understand a short review or interview.

10 Celebrations

In this unit you will learn how to:
▶ *make arrangements and plans.*
▶ *accept or decline invitations.*
▶ *write short and simple notes.*
▶ *use comparatives and superlatives to describe and compare events.*

CEFR (A1): Can understand short descriptions and describe celebrations in your own country.

Festivals and national celebrations

Israel celebrates official Jewish festivals as national holidays. The state emblem of Israel is a menorah, a candelabrum with seven branches, surrounded by olive branches. The menorah was used in the holy temple in Biblical times and has become an iconic national symbol of peace.

In Israel, Jewish holidays are observed, for example, the biblical seventh day of the week שבת **Sabbath**, which is the weekly day of rest. Some other festivals have Biblical origins such as *Passover* פסח **Pesach**, the *Feast of Tabernacles* סוכות **Sukkot**, and the *Festival of First Fruit* שבועות **Shavuot**. These three festivals are known as the pilgrimage festivals. Other holidays commemorate stories that originated later in Jewish history, such as the *Festival of Light* חנוכה **Chanukah**, and פורים **Purim**, *the Festival of Disguises*, as well as *Independence Day* יום העצמאות **Yom Ha'atzmaut**.

The main two fast days are the *Biblical Day of Atonement* יום כיפור **Yom Kippur**, and the *Ninth of Av* תשעה באב **Tishah B'av**, which commemorates the destruction of the Jewish Temple in Jerusalem.

Can you identify the Hebrew or English names of the holidays described?

Vocabulary builder

 10.01 **Listen and repeat these words relating to festivals, occasions, and celebrations.**

FESTIVALS

חג	חג	chag	*festival*
שבת	שבת	shabbat	*Saturday*
ראש השנה	ראש-השנה	rosh-hashana	*Rosh-hashana (head of the year)*
סוכות	סוכות	sukkah	*Sukkah (tabernacles)*
פסח	פסח	pesach	*Passover*
צום	צום	tzom	*fast*
נרות	נרות	nerot	*candles*

OCCASIONS

חתונה	חתונה	chatuna	*wedding*
בר-מצווה	בר-מצווה	bar-mitzvah	*bar mitzvah*
יום הולדת	יום הולדת	yom-huledet	*birthday*
חגיגת יום הולדת	חגיגת יום הולדת	chagigat yom huledet	*birthday party*
הזמנה	הזמנה	hazmana	*invitation*
להזמין	להזמין	lehazmin	*to invite*
מוזמן	מוזמן	muzman (m/s)	*invited*
מצטער	מצטער	mitztaer (m/s)	*sorry*
שמח	שמח	same'ach (m/s)	*happy*
מתנצל	מתנצל	mitnatzel (m/s)	*apologies*
חבר חברה חברים	חבר, חברה, חברים	chaver (m/s) chavera (f/s) chaverim	*friend / friends*
שיר / שירים	שיר / שירים	shir / shirim	*song / songs*
ריקוד /ריקודים	ריקוד / ריקודים	rikud / rikudim	*dance / dances*

NEW EXPRESSIONS

לשנה הבאה בירושלים לשנה הבאה	לשנה הבאה בירושלים	Leshana haba'ah Byrushalayim.	*Next year in Jerusalem.*
שלום שבת.	שבת שלום.	Shabbat shalom.	*Have a good Sabbath.*
שמח חג.	חג שמח.	Chag same'ach.	*Happy holiday.*
טובה שנה.	לחיים!	Shana tova.	*Happy new year.*

לחיים!	*יום הולדת שמח*	Lechayim!	Cheers!
שמח הולדת יום	*מזל טוב*	Yom Huledet Sameach!	Happy birthday!
טוב מזל	*לא יכול*	Mazal tov!	Congratulations!
יכול לא	*לא בא*	lo yachol (m/s)	can not
בא לא	*יהודים*	lo ba (m/s)	don't come
יהודים	*נוצרים*	Yehudim	Jews
נוצרים	*מוסלמים*	Notzrim	Christians
מוסלמים	*מוסלמים*	Muslemim	Muslims

VERBS

to invite	להזמין		**lehazmin**
m/s	מזמין		**mazmin**
f/s	מזמינה		**mazmina**
m/p	מזמינים		**mazminim**
f/p	מזמינות		**mazminot**
to apologize	להתנצל		**lehitnatzel**
m/s	מתנצל		**mitnatzel**
f/s	מתנצלת		**mitnatzelet**
m/p	מתנצלים		**mitnatzlim**
f/p	מתנצלות		**mitnatzlot**
to come	לבוא		**lavo**
m/s	בא		**ba**
f/s	באה		**ba'a**
m/p	באים		**baeim**
f/p	באות		**baot**
can			
m/s	יכול		**yachol**
f/s	יכולה		**yechola**
m/p	יכולים		**yecholim**
f/p	יכולות		**yecholot**

> **TIP**
> *Cannot* is expressed in Hebrew as *not can*: לא יכול.

Conversation and comprehension 1

10.02 *Rosh Hashana and Pesach are two festivals where families gather together. Listen to the following conversation between a mother and her married daughter.*

 Can you change the conversation between mother and daughter to a conversation between mother and son?

Mother	Hi, ma shlomech?	?היי, מה שלומך
Daughter	Tov, toda.	.טוב, תודה
Mother	Atem chogegim babayit Shelanu Hashana?	?אתם חוגגים בבית שלנו השנה
Daughter	Mitztaeret ima, hashana Anachnu im hahorim shel Eitan.	מצטערת אימא, השנה אנחנו עם ההורים של איתן.
Mother	Aval hashana kol hamishpacha Chogegim babayit shelanu. Anachnu mazminim gam etchem.	אבל השנה כול המשפחה חוגגת בבית שלנו. אנחנו מזמינים גם אתכם.
Daughter	Gam hamishpacha shel eitan mazminim otanu.	גם המשפחה של איתן מזמינים אותנו.
Mother	Beshana haba'a atem. Chogegim babayit shelanu?	בשנה הבאה אתם חוגגים בבית שלנו?
Daughter	Ken ima, chag same'ach, le'hitraot!	!כן אימא, חג שמח, להתראות

1 Answer these questions.
  a What is the name of the daughter's husband?
  b Where is the daughter celebrating this year?
  c Where is the couple celebrating next year?

2 Match the two columns with the related or opposite words.
  a Rosh hashana ראש השנה
  b Toda תודה
  c Pesach פסח
  d Ben בן
  e Shalom שלום

  1 Bevakasha בבקשה
  2 Chag same'ach חג שמח
  3 Shana tova שנה טובה
  4 Lehitraot להתראות
  5 Bat בת

> **TIP**
> The origin of the word *festival*, חג **chag** is in the Bible. It is related to the pilgrimage festivals. The Muslim pilgrimage, which is one of the five pillars of Islam, is called **chaj** חאג'.

Language discovery

Read through the conversation again. The words that are used instead of *celebrate with us* or *celebrate with them* are *at our home* and *at their home*. Remember, you learned the words *our* שלנו and *their* שלהם in Unit 6.

WITH US / WITH THEM

איתי	**איתי** itee	*with me*		איתנו	**איתנו** itanu	*with us*
איתך	**איתך** itcha	*with you (m/s)*		איתכם	**איתכם** itchem	*with you*
איתך	**איתך** itach	*with you (f/s)*		איתכן	**איתכן** itchen	*with you*
איתו	**איתו** ito	*with him (m/s)*		איתם	**איתם** itam	*with them*
איתה	**איתה** ita	*with her (f/s)*		איתן	**איתן** itan	*with them*

1 **Choose the Hebrew word from the following that matches the underlined phrases.**

   a She goes <u>with him</u>.   **1** איתי
   b They celebrate <u>with us</u>.   **2** איתך (m/s)
   c He is chatting <u>with me</u>.   **3** איתך (f/s)
   d He is going <u>with her</u>.   **4** איתו
   e We are celebrating <u>with them</u> (f/p).   **5** איתה
   f I talk <u>with you</u> (m/s) on the phone.   **6** איתנו
   g We celebrate <u>with you</u> (m/p).   **7** איתכם
   h They go <u>with them</u> (m/p) to Israel.   **8** איתכן
   i They like chatting <u>with you</u> (f/s).   **9** איתם
   j He wants to play <u>with you</u> (f/p).   **10** איתן

2 10.03 **Listen and respond to the following questions with yes or no answers. Use the first two examples provided as your guide.**

a אתה רוצה ללכת איתי?   כן, אני רוצה ללכת איתך

b אתה רוצה ללכת איתי?   כן, אני רוצה ללכת איתך

c אתם הולכים לדיסקו?

d היא חוגגת את הפסח איתכם?

e את רוצה לבוא איתנו לחגיגת יום - הולדת?

INFLECTIONS

You have already learned some Hebrew inflections. Take a moment to revise these.

	אני	*אני*	ani	*I*	איתי	*איתי*	iti	*with me*
m/s	אתה	*אתה*	ata	*you*	איתך	*איתך*	itcha	*with you*
f/s	את	*את*	at	*you*	איתך	*איתך*	itach	*with you*
	הוא	*הוא*	hu	*he*	איתו	*איתו*	ito	*with him*
	היא	*היא*	hee	*she*	איתה	*איתה*	ita	*with her*
	אנחנו	*אנחנו*	anachnu	*we*	איתנו	*איתנו*	itanu	*with us*
m/p	אתם	*אתם*	atem	*you*	איתכם	*איתכם*	itchem	*with you*
f/p	אתן	*אתן*	aten	*you*	איתכן	*איתכן*	itchen	*with you*
m/p	הם	*הם*	hem	*they*	איתם	*איתם*	itam	*with them*
f/p	הן	*הן*	hen	*they*	איתן	*איתן*	itan	*with them*

POSSESIVE PRONOUNS

	לי	*לי*	li	*to me*	שלי	*שלי*	sheli	*my*
m/s	לך	*לך*	lecha	*to you*	שלך	*שלך*	shelcha	*your*
f/s	לך	*לך*	lach	*to you*	שלך	*שלך*	shelach	*your*
	לו	*לו*	lo	*to him*	שלו	*שלו*	shelo	*his*
f/s	לה	*לה*	la	*to her*	שלה	*שלה*	shela	*her*
	לנו	*לנו*	lanu	*to us*	שלנו	*שלנו*	shelanu	*our*
m/p	לכם	*לכם*	lachem	*to you*	שלכם	*שלכם*	shelachem	*your*
f/p	לכן	*לכן*	lichen	*to you*	שלכן	*שלכן*	shelachen	*your*
m/p	להם	*להם*	lahem	*to them*	שלהם	*שלהם*	shelahem	*their*
f/p	להן	*להן*	lahen	*to them*	שלהן	*שלהן*	shelahen	*their*

Conversation and comprehension 2

10.04 Ben and Ruth are discussing how they would like to celebrate Independence Day.

1 Will they be celebrating together?

Ben	Ani ohev chagiga im shirim verikudim yisre'elim.	אני אוהב חגיגה עם שירים וריקודים ישראליים.
Ruth	Ken, ze yafe meod, aval ani ma'adifa chagigat yom ha'atzmaut im Chverim leyad habarbecue.	כן, זה יפה מאוד, אבל אני מעדיפה חגיגת יום העצמאות עם חברים ליד הברביקיו.
Ben	Ani rotze linsoa lekibutz, sham anachnu chogegim beshirim verikudim ad haboker.	אני רוצה לנסוע לקיבוץ, שם אנחנו חוגגים בשירים וריקודים עד הבוקר.
Ruth	Ani holechet labayit shel Rachel veDavid. Anachnu chogegim leyad habarbecue im chaverim. Sham anachnu shotim lechayim lichvod Yisrael.harbe kosot lechayim.	אני הולכת לבית של רחל ודויד. אנחנו חוגגים ליד הברביקיו עם חברים. שם אנחנו שותים לחיים לכבוד ישראל. הרבה כוסות לחיים.
Ben	Chag same'ach!	חג שמח!
Ruth	Chag same'ach gam lecha!	חג שמח!

2 Answer the following questions.
   a Where do people go singing and dancing to celebrate?
   b Does Ruth object to drinking wine?
   c How do you say *Happy holiday* in Hebrew?

 Can you see a relationship between the endings of the singular and plural pronouns and their inflections?

 Reading and writing

1 You have learned that Jewish festivals and celebrations have their own specific greetings and blessings. Can you match the correct celebration with the greeting that would be given?
   a בר מצווה (bar-mitzvah) _____
   b פסח (Passover) _____
   c חתונה (wedding) _____

d סוכות (sukkot, tabernacles) _____

e יום הולדת (birthday)_____

f ראש השנה (rosh hashana) _____

1 חג שמח

2 מזל טוב

3 שנה טובה

4 יום הולדת שמח

2 Use the words below to fill in this invitation to the wedding of דפנה מיכאל and.

אנחנו _____ להזמין אתכם, ל_____, של

דפנה (Daphne) ומיכאל (Michael),

ביום שני, 15.3.13 ב_____ ב 19.00 _____

הילטון ב _____

חתונה שעה מלון תל-אביב מזמינים

3 Fill in the RSVP by first accepting and then declining the invitation. Use the words listed below.

אנחנו ._____ תודה על	_____ על ההזמנה.
שאנחנו _____	שמחים לבוא ל_____
לבוא לחתונה,	._____
טוב _____	

_____ תודה על שמחים _____	_____ על ההזמנה.
שאנחנו לא יכולים _____ אנחנו	לבוא ל _____.
לחתונה. _____	_____
טוב! _____	

אנחנו, חתונה, תודה, להתראות | ההזמנה, מזל, מצטערים, לבוא

Test yourself

Translate these festive greetings and phrases into English.

1. ‫טובה שנה.‬

2. ‫מצווה בר חוגגים אנחנו.‬

3. ‫טוב מזל, לחיים.‬

4. ‫מוסיקה יש שלנו בחגיגה.‬

5. ‫אתכם מזמינה שלנו המשפחה.‬

SELF CHECK

I CAN. . .

. . . make plans and arrangements and accept or decline invitations.
. . . name the key festivals and provide the appropriate blessing.
. . . use comparatives and superlatives to describe and compare events.

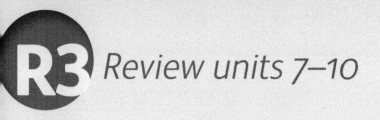

PRONOUNS

1 **Complete the following with personal and possessive pronouns. Use the Hebrew table to help you if required.**

I	אני	my	שלי	to me	לי...	with me	איתי
you (m/s)	אתה	your (m/s)	שלך	to you (m/s)	לך	with you	איתך
you (f/s)		your (f/s)		to you (f/s)			
he		his		to him			
she		her		to her			
we		our		us			
you (m/p)		your (m/p)		to you (m/p)			
you (f/p)		your (f/p)		to you (f/s)			
they (m/p)		their (m/p)		to them			
they (f/p)		their (f/p)		to them			

אני	אתה	את	הוא	היא	אנחנו	אתם	אתן	הם	הן
שלי	שלך (m/s)	שלך (f/s)	שלו (m/s)	שלה (f/s)	שלנו	שלכם (m/p)	שלכן (f/p)	שלהם (m/p)	שלהן (m/f)
לי	לך (m/s)	לך (f/s)	לו (m/s)	לה (f/s)	לנו	לכם (m/p)	לכן (f/p)	להם (m/p)	להן (f/p)
איתי	איתך (m/s)	איתך (f/s)	איתו (m/s)	איתה (f/s)	איתנו	איתכם (m/p)	איתכן (f/p)	איתם	איתן

2 Read the letter Rose wrote to her friend David.

20 January	בינואר 20
Hi David	שלום דויד
How are you? We are in Israel, in a hotel in Jerusalem. I'm enjoying going on trips and hikes to museums and concerts, to the cinema, and eating in great restaurants. On Sunday I am going to see my family in Tel-Aviv and on Thursday I have to fly to England.	מה שלומך? אני בישראל, במלון בירושלים. אני אוהבת לטייל, ללכת למוזיאון, לקונצרטים, לקולנוע, ולאכול במסעדה טובה.
	ביום ראשון אני עם המשפחה שלי בתל-אביב, וביום חמישי אני צריכה לטוס לאנגליה.
Shabbat Shalom,	שבת שלום,
Kisses, Rose	נשיקות, רח.

a Looking at the Hebrew letter, what is the English translation of the Hebrew words that follow. You can use the glossary at the end of this book to help.

נשיקות, משפחה, מסעדה, מלון, אנחנו.

b If the letter was written by David, and to Rose, which words in the Hebrew letter would need to be changed?

3 Translate the following passage into English.

ערב. מה הם רוצים לאכול? הכול!
יש לי משפחה גדולה. הם באים לארוחת
ערב תעוגה! הם לא בדיאטה. בתיאבון!
סטייק, סלט, ספגטי, צ'יפס, וגם קפה

Yesh li mishpacha gdola. Hem ba'im learuchat erev. Ma hem rotzim le'echol? Hakol. Steak, salat, spaghetti, chips, vegam kafe veuga. Hem lo bete'avon.

PARTICLES

4 Complete these sentences using the words and phrases provided.

  a יש _____ משפחה גדולה

  b ערב לארוחת באים _____

  c _____ לאכול רוצים הם?

  d בדיאטה _____ הם

מה 4 לי 3 הם 2 לא 1

5 Choose words from the box, and add them to the correct sentence, according to the subjects and themes suggested.

> בלט, ג'ודו, רמזור, מטוס, קונצרט, סרט, רכבת, רחוב, צ'יפס, שינה חדר, כדורסל,
> מטבח, פארק, סקסי, סלט, אורחים חדר, שחייה, אופרה, אוטובוס, שניצל

  a דויד אוהב ספורט: כדורגל, _____

  b בבית של רות יש: חדר אוכל, _____

  c אנחנו אוכלים: סטייק, _____

  d יש בעיר: בית כנסת, _____

  e (transportation)תחבורה: _____

  f אנחנו הולכים לתיאטרון _____

6 Choose the correct use of each word following the name, noun or personal pronoun.

a עובדת / עובד – רחל

b קטנה / קטן – בית

c קטנה / גדול – פארק

d אדומה / אדום – רמזור

e נוסעת / נוסע – רכבת

f קטנה / קטן – מכונית

g גרה / גר – דן

h חוגגים / חוגגת – אנחנו

7 Complete the crossword puzzle in Hebrew.

HORIZONTAL:

1 Bath **2** Money **5** Comedy **8** Tea **10** Mail **12** The glass

13 His **14** Date **18** Yes **20** Grandfather **22** Just, only **23** Come (m/s)

VERTICAL:

1 Sister **2** Bank **3** How much, how many **4** Passover **6** Shower **7** beautiful
9 Go (m/s) **11** Green **15** Father **16** Go out (m/s) **17** Expensive **19** Candle
21 Come (m/s)

Answer key

PRONUNCIATION

Practice 1

א	ב	ב	ג	ד	ה	ו	ז	ח	ט	י
a	b	v	g	d	h	v	z	ch	T	y

Practice 3

כּ	כ	ל	מ	נ	ס	ע	בּ	פ	צ	ק	ר	שׁ	שׂ	ת
k	ch	ל	m	n	s	a	P	ph	tz	k	r	sh	s	t

UNIT 1

Practice 1

1 Match the Hebrew letters to their English equivalent.

א = a; ב = b; ג = g; ד = d; ה = h; ו = v; ז = z; ח = ch; ט = t; י = y

Practice 3

Match the Hebrew letter to the English equivalent.

נ = n; ח = t; ס = s; ע = a; פּ = p; פ = f; צ = ch '; ט = st; ק = k; ר = r; שׂ = sh; שׁ = s; ת = t;
כּ = k; כ = ch; ל = l; מ = m;

Welcome!

Capital city of Israel is Jerusalem; Nazareth; Bethlehem

Vocabulary builder

a Good evening, **b** Good night, **c** Good morning, **d** hello,
e until next time

Conversation and comprehension

1 They meet in the morning.

2 **a** נעים מאה. **e** אתה מבין אנגלית? **d** מי אתה? **c** להתראות! **b** אתה מדבר אנגלית?
f בוקר טוב

4 **a**1, **b**4, **c**2, **d**5, **e**3, **f**6

Listen and understand

1 **a** Ani medaber Anglit? **b** Ani medaber Ivrit. **c** Ata Mevin? **d** Ata rotze te o kafe?

3 **a** m/s, **b** f/p, **c** mp, **d** m/f/p, **e** f/s

4 **a** טוב(tov) **b** מי (mee) **c** אני (ani) **d** טוב (tov) **e** מדבר(medaber)
f אני (ani) **g** עברית (ivrit) **h** מבינה (mevina)
5 **a.**_____ אני קפה רוצה אני, כן **c** קפה רוצה לא אני, לא **d** תודה, טוב

Practice

1 All verbs are in this order: m/s f/s m/p f/p
2 **a** גרה **e** אבל מ ... **c** ו... **d** ל ... **b** וגם
3 **a** גר **b** נוסעת **c** רוצה **d** גם **e** הוא

Test yourself

1 **a**2, **b**3, **c**1, **d**4
2 **a** נוסעת **b** מדבר **c** רוצה **d** גר **e** מבינה לא
3 **a** to **b** from **c** in **d** and
4 **a** איתי **e** אתן **d** אנחנו, אתם **c** אני, את **b** אני, אתה

UNIT 2

The Israeli family

a father **b** mother **c** son **d** grandmother

Conversation and comprehension 1

1 His grandfather and his mother. **2** His mother is 40 years old.
3 His grandparents live in Israel.

Listen and understand

2 **a**2, **b**4, **c**1, **d**3
3 Their – שלהם our – שלנו

Practice

1 **a**4, **b**3, **c**2, **d**1, **e**5
2 **a** שלכם **b** שלנו **c** שלהן

Conversation and comprehension 2:

1 What does David's mother look like?
2 **a** f/s, **b** f/p, **c** s/m, **d** s/m, **e** s/f, **f** f/p, **g**m/p
3 At Rotza Kafe? את רוצה קפה?
4 **a**. Eilat **b**. Jerusalem **c**. in the morning **d**. grandmother **e**. Yes

Learn more

1 מדברת מדברים מדברות
2 In the verb 'to live' only two root-letters appear in the verb inflections.

Reading and writing

1 **a** אימא **e** אימא **d** בת **c** בן **b** סבא **a** אבא
2 **a** זה **b** גר **c** גדולה **d** בן **e** יפה
3 **a** גר **e** גדול **d** קטנה **c** טובה **b** נמוכה

Test yourself

My family is large. Mother, father, two grandfathers and two grandmothers. I have two brothers and three sisters. My brothers are tall and good-looking and my sisters are short and beautiful.

UNIT 3
Vocabulary builder

Missing words: malon - hotel, טלפון – telephone, מייל – email, טלוויזיה - television

1 במלון in the hotel; בחדר in the room
2 או
3 חדר עם מזגן

Conversation and comprehension

1 7 days
2 television, telephone, bath, June.
3 It will be a big room, with a bathroom, television, telephone.
4 Female.

Language discovery

1 a אני מבקש b. להזמין
2 a and b or c from
4 a שולחות b רוצים c מבקשת d מזמין e שולח
7 a מבין b עובדת c רוצים d שולח e מבקש f מדבר
8 a אין b מזמין c לא מבין d לא שולח e לא יפה f לא רוצה g לא מדבר h קטן

Speaking

(answers in affirmative and negative in brackets).

2 a כן (לא) אני (אני לא) גר במלון
b כן (לא) אני (אני לא) רוצה לגור במלון
c אני נוסע לטייל (...) בדצמבר, ינואר

Test yourself

2 a להזמין b מבקש c לשלוח d ימים e מתי f עובד g מצטער h מאוד

REVIEW UNITS 1–3

1 a f/s b f/s c m/p d f/p e m/s f f/p g m/s h m/p i f/s j f/s
2 a פני ו f גדולה e קטנים d קטן c רחב b יפות
3 a my = שלי; b your (m/s) = שלך; c your (f/s) = שלך; d his = שלו;
e her = שלה; f our = שלנו; g your (m/p) = שלכם; h your (f/p) = שלכן;
i their (m/p) = שלהם; j their (f/p) = שלהן
5 a2 b3 c6 d4 e7 f5 g8 h10 i9 j1

6

M/S	גר	מזמין	מדבר	מבקש	מבין
F/S	גרה	מזמינה	מדברת	מבקשת	מבינה
M/P	גרים	מזמינים	מדברים	מבקשים	מבינים
F/P	גרות	מזמינות	מדברות	מבקשות	מבינות

7

Discovery question: Book of Exodus (3, 8) & Book of Deuteronomy (6, 3)

a We speak Hebrew.

b Dan is traveling from Tel-Aviv to Jerusalem.

c Do you want coffee or tea?

d Our rooms are large.

e My mother is beautiful.

8

a אני מדבר (מדברת) אנגלית

b המשפחה שלי גרה בתל-אביב

c החדר הזה יפה

d יש לנו משפחה גדולה

e המייל שלי: ronb@gmail.com

UNIT 4

Israeli fashion

Jeans and t-shirt and the same in Hebrew as in English.

Vocabulary builder

1 חנויות = חנות, מחירים = מחיר, שמלות= שמלה, חולצות = חולצה

2 They are pairs.

Conversation and comprehension

1 Mrs Brown thinks the dress is expensive.

2 שמלה יפה, שמלה יפה חולה

3 Yes, she did. **4** Yes, it does.

5 a3; b4; c1; d5; e2

6 a3, b1, c4, d2

Learn more

1 **a** 16, **b** 14, **c** 19, **d** 20, **e**12

3 **a** 222, **b** 115, **c** 432, **d** 972, **e** 785, **f** 1125

Listen and understand

1

a I ask for a yellow shirt,

b The dress is too short.

c The dress costs 400 ₪.

d The suit is cheap.

2 a 300 **b** 125 **c** 15 **d** 7 **e** 201 **f** 4 **g** 13 **h** 27

Conversation and comprehension 2

The mother buys 3 items of clothing.

1 האמא מסכימה לקנות את הבגדים

2 Four colours are mentioned in the conversation.

4

a Can I help you?

b What size fits?

c I prefer a white shirt.

d How much does it cost?

e I want two cheap shirts

f I am not buying because it is too expensive.

g Mom buys clothes with Dan.

Practice

1

adjective	m/s	f/s	m/p	f/p
Fit	מתאים	מתאימה	מתאימים	מתאימות
Big	גדול	גדולה	גדולים	גדולות
Small	קטן	קטנה	קטנים	קטנות
Short	קצר	קצרה	קצרים	קצרות
Long	ארוך	ארוכה	ארוכים	ארוכות
Cheap	זול	זולה	זולים	זולות
expensive	יקר	יקרה	יקרים	יקרות

2

a The sea is כחול.

b The grass is ירוק.

c When the traffic lights are אדום stop!

d The sun is צהוב.

e שחור as night.

f The colours of the Israeli flag are <u>לבן</u> and <u>כחול</u>.

Test yourself

1 It costs 500 Shekels

2 20 + 50 = 70

3 Beautiful green suit

4 Suitable blue shirt

5 At the end of the season the clothes are cheap

UNIT 5

The Israeli flag

מגן-דוד אדום

Vocabulary builder

a זמן

b נהיגה

c טס

d טקסי, אוטובוס, אוטו

Conversation and comprehension 1

1 The Greens are going to Tel-Aviv Return Fare costs 45 Shekels

2 The bus stands on platform 3.

3 The bus leaves at 12 o'clock.

4 **a**3; **b**4; **c**5; **d**1; **e**2

Language discovery

1f; **2**b; **3**e; **4**c; **5**a; **6**d

Listen and understand

1

a מתי הרכבת יוצאת?

b הטקסי נוסע לאילת

c הרכבת מגיעה לתחנה

d נסיעה טובה

e איפה רציף 3?

f אפשר לעזור לך?

2

a יוצא

b The train leaves from platform **3**.

c The bus goes to תל-אביב.

d They buy their tickets at the קופה.

e I drive a מכונית.

3

a תל-אביב

b קופה

c מכונית (אוטו)

3

a From Ben-Gurion airport.

b He wants to go to England.

c He bought a return ticket.

d He leaves on the 10th July and comes back on the 17th.

e Five o'clock in the evening

Conversation and comprehension 2

a כמה זה עולה?

b אפשר לעזור לך?

c It is hired for a week.

d They ask for a small car.

e It costs 35 Shekels

Practice

1 תחנה / כרטיס / טייס / רציף / אוטובוס / נהג / לשכור / אוטו / רכבת / לנסוע

2 **a** רישיון-נהיגה **g** שוב **f** לך **e** בבע **d** קטנה **c** רכבת **b** תחנה

Test yourself

I want to go (fly) to England next week, Tuesday at 7 o'clock to visit my family.

UNIT 6

Getting around Israel

Nazareth – נצרת   sea - ים   mountain – הר

Vocabulary builder

1 1. רחוב 7. פינה 6. בית כנסת 5. בית ספר 4. חנות 3. דואר 2. סופרמרקט

2 **a** bank

   b post office

   c shop

   d school

   e synagogue

   f corner

   g street

Conversation and comprehension 1

1 **a** false **b** true **c** false **d** true

2 **a**3 **b**1 **c**4 **d**5 **e**2

3 a זה לא רחוק

 b איפה ה...?

 c זה ליד ה...

 d מול

Language Discovery

1 a beautiful museum **b** the map **c** the street **d** traffic-lights **e** the big park **f** the beautiful church **g** the bank

2 ימינה; צפונה; דרומה

3 a הולך שמאלה **b** ברחוב **c** במזרח **d** ליד הבנק

Practice

1 בית כנסת; כנסייה; בית ספר; רמזור

3

a המפה	**b** הרמזור	**c** ברחוב
d המוזיאון היפה	**e** מול הבנק	

Practice 2

2 a Sarah turns right

 b I walk in the street

 c Where is it possible to change money?

 d The bank is near the park.

 e The synagogue in Ben Gurion Street.

3 a דרומה **b** פינה **c** רחוב **d** הדואר **e** רחוק **f** את

4 a In Israel

 b Yes

 c Yes

 d Sunday 30th of September.

Conversation and comprehension 2

1 נצרת, חיפה, מצדה נצרת, אילת

2 To visit historic places, museums, go to the theatre and to classical music concerts.

3 They live in Tel-Aviv and Jerusalem.

4 Bon voyage!

Test yourself

1 Tom turns to the right.

2 Where is the beautiful park?

3 The red house near the synagogue.

4 The school opposite the bank.

5 Ron goes (travels) to the south.

REVIEW UNITS 4–6

1 **a** גדולים/יקרים ימכנסיים

b שמלה – צהובה, ירוקה, יקרה, גדולה, קטנה

c חולצות – זולות

d רחוב – גדול, יפה, קרוב,

e כרטיסים – גדולים, יקרים,

f מחזאון – גדול, יפה, קרוב,

g מפה – צהובה, גדולה, קטנה

h חולצה – צהובה, גדולה, קטנה

i פארק – גדול, יפה, קרוב

3 חולצה ירוקה

רמזור צהוב

מכנסיים אדומים

שמלה כחולה

בגדים לבנים

חולצות שחורות

a. שמונה ורבע

b. שתים עשרה וחצי

c. חמש דקות לאחת עשרה

d. עשר דקות לארבע

e. שבע ושלושים

f. שש ארבעים וחמש

g. שתים עשרה ורבע

5

Root	ד.ל.ה	ע.ס.ג	ג.ה.ג	ה.צ.ר
m/s	הולך	נוסע	נוהג	רוצה
f/s	הולכת	נוסעת	נוהגת	רוצה
m/p	הולכים	נוסעים	נוהגים	רוצים
f/p	הולכות	נוסעות	נוהגות	רוצות

7. a. מ...ל... b. ליד / c. ל...ל. d. איפה e. מ...עד / f. ליד / g. מתי h. שלך i. ב...

8 b. this school c. this school d. to the right

9 **a** I am going to school

b He is going to the right

c Is this house yours

d Yes this is my house

e The house next to the big post-office

f Your dress is pretty

g The shirt is red, expensive and beautiful

An Israeli restaurant in London
Book of Exodus (3, 8) & Book of Deuteronomy (6, 3)
שָׁבְדוּ בְלָח תבְנֶ עֶרֶא.

Conversation and comprehension 1

1 Coffee shop/ Patisserie

2 a True **b** False **c** False **d** True **e** True

Language discovery

1 a2, **b**3, **c**1

2 עוד; די ;פחות; רק; זה מספיק ;רק קצת

3 a כן, האוכל טעים

   b כן, בבקשה

   c תה בבקשה

   d כן, בבקשה

   e כן, תודה

4 a The food is very tasty.

   b I eat steak and chips.

   c A glass of beer, please.

   d There is good food on the menu.

   e The food is too salty.

Listen and understand

a no **b** Germany. **c** Falafel and salad in pitta bread. **d** Falafel, salad and schnitzel **e** yes

Conversation and comprehension 2

1 Steak and salad.

2 a Tom drinks white wine.

   b No, Rachel likes her steak 'medium-well',

   c No-one drinks water,

   d La = for her, li = for me,

3 a For me, just

   b Much

   c For him and for her,

   d Ask, for me and for her

4 **a** הבית הזה שלי
b כן, הניטרה הזו שלו
c לא, אין לה אוטו
d לי תה, בבקשה
e לא, הבגד הזה לא שלו

UNIT 8

Working in Israel

חקלאות, רפואה

Vocabulary builder

a4; **b**3; **c**2; **d**5; **e**1; **f**8; **g**6; **h**7

Conversation and comprehension 1

Time of day: it is morning.

1 **a** Nobody **b** No **c** Dan **d** Gets up late

2 **a**4, **b**2, **c**1, **d**3, **e**5

Language discovery

1 Professions: **a** m/p **b** f/p **c** m/s **d** f/p **e** m/p **f** m/s
Nouns: **g** f/s **h** f/s **i** f/p **j** f/s **k** m/p **l** m/s **m** f/p **n** f/p

Listen and understand

a Ruth **b** No **c** At the office **d** Yes **e** At university

Conversation and comprehension 2

1 **a** Rachel can start working at 9 a.m., and Tom should begin later.
  b Rachel, at 7 p.m., Tom – at 8 p.m.
  c Rachel does and Tom doesn't.
  d Rachel, in her dining room, and Tom in the kitchen.
  e Their TV sets stand in the guest room.

2 **a** Study = 6, **b** Bathroom =1, **c** Dining room =5, **d** Kitchen = 2, **e** Bedroom =3, **f** Guest room/ lounge = 4

3 **a**3, **b**1, **c**2, **d**5, **e**4

Test yourself

1 **a** You have to get-up earlier
  b I read in bed-room
  c My father is a policeman
  d They work in the kitchen
  e She wants to be a doctor

2 **a** אני קם מוקדם בבוקר
  b אני שותה קפה בכל יום
  c הערב הוא קורא ספרים

d אנחנו אוכלים בחדר האוכל

e היא אוהבת לראות טלביזיה

UNIT 9

National Theatre of Israel

תיאטרון

Vocabulary builder

basket ball – כדור סל

Conversation and comprehension 1

David and Rose are not going out together.

1 a Cabaret
   b Rose
   c Both have tickets
   d Rose

Language discovery

1 a4, **b**1, **c**2, **d**5, **e**3

2

1D	2B	3E	4A	5C

3 Verb & adverb: א. 1, 2, 3 ב. 1, 2, 3 ג. 3, 4 ד. 1, 2

4 Noun & adjective: א. 1, 3, 4 ב. 1, 3, 4, 5, ג. 2, ד. 1, 3 ה. 2, ו. 1, 3, 4, 5

5

אוהבות f\p	קוראים m\p	טובה f\s	קוראת f\s	הולכת f\s
אוהב m\s	טובים m\p	הצגות f\p		

Listen and understand

1 a false **b** true **c** false **d** false **e** true

2 Profession: actress, Age: 35, Artistic preferences: Movies, ballet, jazz music Dislikes: Opera, Sporting activities: Running and swimming

Conversation and comprehension 2

1 a 2–3 hours **b** We don't know **c** No, he runs as well

2 Arts: a, b, d, e, i Sports: c, f, g, h, j, k

3

a הוא רץ מהר? Negative: לא, הוא לא רץ מהר affirmative: כן, הוא רץ מהר

b יש לך כרטיס? negative: לא, אין לי כרטיס affirmative: כן, יש לי כרטיס

c הוא שחקן טוב? Negative: לא, הוא לא שחקן טוב affirmative: כן, הוא שחקן טוב

d לא, הקופה לא פתוחה (הקופה סגורה) :Negative הקופה פתוחה?
affirmative: כן, הקופה פתוחה.

e לא, אני לא אוהב מוסיקת ג'אז :Negative אתה אוהב מוסיקת ג'אז?
Affirmative: כן, אני אוהב מוסיקת ג'אז.

UNIT 10

Festivals and national celebrations

שבת; פסח; סוכות; שבועות; חנוכה; פורים

Conversation and comprehension 1

1 a Ethan
  b She is celebrating with her husband's family.
  c She will celebrate with her family.

2 1C, **2**A, **3**B, **4**E, **5**D

Language discovery

1 a4, **b**6, **c**1, **d**5, **e**10, **f**2, **g**7, **h**9, **i**3, **j**8

2 כן, היא הולכת איתנו לדיסקו / לא, היא לא הולכת איתנו לדיסקו
כן, היא חוגגת איתנו את הפסח / לא, היא לא חוגגת איתנו את הפסח
כן, אני רוצה לבוא איתכם לחגיגת יום הולדת / לא, אני לא רוצה לבוא איתכם לחגיגת
יום הולדת.

Conversation and comprehension 2

1 No.

2 a In the kibbutz.
  b No, she does not.
  c Chag same'ach.

Reading and writing

1 a2; **b**1; **c**2; **d**1; **e**4; **f**3

2 Invitation: אנחנו שמחים להזמין אתכם לחתונה של מיכאל ודפנה, ביום שני ב-15.3.13
בשעה 19.00 בתל-אביב, במלון הילטון.

3 Accept: תודה על ההזמנה. אנחנו שמחים לבוא לחתונה של מיכאל ודפנה. מזל טוב,
ולהתראות.

Decline: תודה על ההזמנה. אנחנו מצטערים שאנחנו לא יכולים לבוא לחתונה. מזל טוב.

Test yourself

1 Happy New Year. **2** We celebrate Bar mitzvah. **3** Cheers, good luck.
4 There is music at our party. **5** Our family invites you.

1

I	אני	my	שלי	to me	...לי	with me	איתי
you (m/s)	אתה	your (m/s)	שלך	to you (m/s)	לך	with you	איתך
you (f/s)	את	your (f/s)	שלך	to you (f/s)	לך	with you	איתך
he	הוא	his	שלו	to him	לו	with him	איתו
she	היא	her	שלה	to her	לה	with her	איתה
we	אנחנו	our	שלנו	us	לנו	with us	איתנו
you (m/p)	אתם	your (m/p)	שלכם	to you (m/p)	לכם	with you	איתכם
you (f/p)	אתן	your (f/p)	שלכן	to you(f/s)	לכן	with you	איתכן
they (m/p)	הם	their (m/p)	שלהם	to them	להם	with them	איתם
they (f/p)	הן	their (f/p)	שלהן	to them	להן	with them	איתן

2 **a** Kisses = נשיקות; **Family** = משפחה; **Restaurant** = מסעדה; **Hotel** = מלון, **We** = אנחנו

   b שלום רח / מה שלומך? / אני אוהב / אני צריך / דויד

3 I have a big family. They come to eat dinner. What do they want to eat? Everything! Steak, salad, spaghetti, chips and also coffee and cake. They are not on a diet. Bon appetite!

4 **a**3, **b**2, **c**4, **d**1

5

a כדורסל, שחייה

b חדר שינה, מטבח, חדר אורחים

c סלט, שניצל

d רחוב, פארק

e מטוס, רכבת, טקסי, אוטובוס

f בלט, סרט, אופרה

6

a עובדת

b קטן

c גדול

d אדום

e נוסעת

f קטנה

g גר

h חוגגים

א1	מ	ב2	ט	י	ה	■	כ3	ס	פ4
ח	■	נ	■	■	■	■	מ	■	ס
ו	■	ק5	ו	מ6	ד	י7	ה	■	ח
ת8	ה9	■	■	ק	■	פ	■	ה10	■
■	מ11	י12	י	ל	■	ה13	כ	ו	ס
■	■	ר	■	ח	■	■	■	ל	■
ש14	ל	ו	ת15ח	א16	ר	י17	כ	■	■
■	■	ק	■	■	ב	■	ו	■	י18
ג19	ר20	■	ס21	ב22	א	■	צ	■	ק
■	ק23	ר	■	א	■	ב24	א	■	ר

4.1 החיש, ודו'ג, לסרודכ

4.2 חבטמ, סיחרוא רדח, הניש רדח

4.3 טלס, לצינש, ספי'צ

4.4 בוחר, קראפ, רוזמר

4.5 סובוטוא, תבכר, יסקט, וטא

4.6 הרפוא, סלב, טרצנוק, סרס

5.1 תעסונ תבכר 5.5 סנדא רוזמר 5.4 לודג קראפ 5.3 וטק תיב 5.2 תדבוע לחר

5.6 סיגגוח ונחנא 5.8 רג וד 5.7 הנטק תינוכמ

Hebrew–English glossary

Conventions

adj adjective; f feminine; m masculine; n noun; v verb; p plural; s singular

אבא	aba	father
אבל	aval	but
אדום	adom	red
אוגוסט	Ogust	August
אוהב	ohev	love (m/s)
אוטו	oto	car
אוטובוס	otobus	bus
אוכל	ochel	food
אולימפיאדה	Olympiada	Olympiad (s/m)
אוניברסיטה	universita	university
אוסטרליה	Ostralia	Australia
אופרה	opera	opera
אוקטובר	October	October
אח	ach	brother
אחד	echad	one (m)
אחד עשר	ached asar	eleven (m)
אחות	achot	sister, nurse
אחת	achat	one (f)
אחת עשרה	achat esre	eleven (f)
איזה	eize	what, which (m)
איזו	eizo	what, which (f)
אילת	Eilat	Eilat (town)
אימא	ima	mother
אימון	imun	training
אין	Ein...	There is no...

אינטרנט	Internet	Internet
איפה	eifo	where
איש(ה)	ish (isha)	man (woman)
אירופה	Eiropa	Europe
אמבטיה	ambatia	bath
אמריקה	America	America
אנגלית	Anglit	English (language)
אנחנו	anachnu	we
אני	ani	I (am) (m & f)
אסיה	Asia	Asia
אפריל	April	April
אפריקה	Africa	Africa
אפשר	efshar	possible
אפשר לעזור?	Efshar la'azor?	May I help?
ארבע	arba	four (f)
ארבע עשרה	arba esre	fourteen (f)
ארבעה	arba'a	four (m)
ארבעה עשר	arba'a asar	fourteen (m)
ארבעים	arbaeim	forty
ארוחה	arucha	meal
ארוחת בוקר	aruchat boker	breakfast
ארוחת ערב	aruchat erev	dinner, supper
ארוחת צהריים	aruchat tzohorayim	lunch
ארוך	aa	long
ארץ	eretz	country
את	et	the
את	at	you (f/s)
אתה	ata	you (m/s)
אתם	atem	you (m/p)
אתן	aten	you (f/p)
ב...	be (like better)	in
בא	bah	come (m/s)

בבקשה	bevakasha	please
בגד	bèged	cloth
בגדים	b'gadim	clothes
בוקר	boker	morning
בוקר טוב	boker tov	gGood morning
בית	bayit	home, house
בית כנסת	beit kneset	synagogue
בית לחם	Beyt lechem	Bethlehem
בית ספר	beyt sefer	school
בלט	balet	ballet
בלרינה	ballerina	ballerina
במה	bama	stage
בן	ben	son, boy
בנק	bank	bank
בקשה	bakasha	request
בר	bar	bar
בר-מצווה	bar-mitzvah	bar mitzvah
בת	bat	daughter, girl
בתאבון	beteavon	bon appétit

גבוה	gavoha	tall, high m
גדול	gadol	big m
ג'ודו	judo	judo
גיטרה	guitar	guitar
ג'יפ	jeep	jeep
ג'אז	jazz	jazz
ג'ירף	giraffe	giraffe
גם	gam	too, as well
גר	gar	live, dwell (m)

דואר	doar	post
דולר	dollar	dollar
די	die	enough

דיאטה	dieta	diet
דצמבר	December	December
דקה	daka	minute
דקות	dakot	minutes
ה...	ha	the
הבא	haba	the next, upcoming (m/s)
הוא	hoo	he
הולך	holech	go (m/s)
הזמנה	hazmana	invitation
היא	hee	she
היי-טק	high-Tec	high-tech
הלוך ושוב	haloch vashov	return (ticket)
הליקופטר	helicopter	helicopter
הם	hem	they (m)
הן	hen	they (f)
הנה ה...	Hine ha...	Here is the...
הצגה	show	show
הרבה	harbe	much, many
ו...	ve...	and
ורוד	varod	pink
זברה	zebra	zebra
זה	ze	this, that (m/s)
זו (זאת)	zo, zot	this, that (f/s)
זוג	zug	couple
זול	zol	cheap
זמן	zman	time
חבר	chaver	friend
חג	chag	festival
חג שמח	chag-sameach	happy holiday

חגיגה	chagiga	party
חגיגת יום-הולדת	chagigat yom huledet	birthday party
חדר	cheder	room
חדר אוכל	chadar ochel	dining room
חדר אורחים	chadar orchim	guest room
חדר זוגי	cheder zugi	double room
חדר כושר	chadar kosher	gym
חדר שינה	chadar sheina	bedroom
חדש	chadash	new (m)
חודש	chodesh	month
חולצה	chultza	shirt
חלב	chalav	milk
חליפה	chalifa	suit
חמישה	chamisha	five (m)
חמישה עשר	chamish asar	fifteen (m)
חמישי	(Yom) Chamishi	fifth (Thursday)
חמישים	chamishim	fifty
חמש	chamesh	five (f)
חמש מאות	chamesh meot	five hundred
חמש עשרה	chamesh esre	fifteen (f)
חנוכה	Chanuka	Hanukah
חנוכייה	Chanukia	Hanukah candelabra
חנות	chanut	shop
חצי	chetzi	half
חקלאי	chaklay	farmer
חתונה	chatuna	wedding
טוב	tov	good
טורקיז	turkiz	turquoise
טיפ	tip	tip
טלביזיה	televizia	television
טלפון	telephon	telephone
סניס	tennis	tennis

טעים	taeem	tasty
טקסי	taxi	taxi
טרגדיה	tragedia	tragedy
טרקטור	tractor	tractor
יהודים	Yehudim	Jews
יולי	Yulee	July
יום	yom	day
יום עבודה	yom avoda	working day
יוני	Yunee	June
יוצא	yotze	goes out (m/s)
יותר	yoter	more
יין	yayin	wine
יכול	yachol	can (m/s)
ימין	yamin	right
ימינה	yamina	to the right
ינואר	Yanuar	January
יפה	yafeh/ ah	beautiful (m/f)
יפו	Yafo	Jaffa
יקר	yakar	expensive (adj)
ירוק	yarok	green
ירושלים	Yerushalayim	Jerusalem
יש	yesh	there is...
יש לי	yesh li	I have
ישראל	Yisrael	Israel
כדורגל	kaduregel	football
כדורסל	kadursal	basketball
כהה	kehe	dark
כול יום	kol yom	every day
כוס	kos	drinking glass
כושר	kosher	fitness
כחול	kachol	blue

כי	kee	because
כול שעה	kol sha'ah	every hour
כמה	Kama?	How much, how many?
כמה זה עולה?	Kama ze ole?	How much does it cost?
כמה זמן?	Kama zman?	How long?
כנסייה	knesia	church
כסף	kesef	money
כרטיס	kartis	ticket
כתום	katom	orange
לא	lo	no
לא אוהב	lo ohev	don't love (m/s)
לא יכול	lo yachol	can't (m/s)
לאחר	le'acher	to be late
לאט	le'at	slowly
לאכול	le'echol	to eat
לאן	Le'an?	Where to?
לבן	lavan	white
לבקש	levakesh	to ask for
לגלוש	liglosh	to surf
להזמין	lehazmin	to order
להחליף	lehachalif	to change
להיות	liheyot	to be
להיט	lahit	hit
להתחיל	lehatchil	to begin
להתראות	lehitraot	see you
לוח זמנים	luach zmanim	timetable
לומד	lomed	study (m/s)
לחיים	lechayim	cheers
לטוס	latus	to fly
לטייל	letayel	to go on a trip
לי	li	to me
ליד	leyad	near the...

לילה	layla	night
לילה טוב	layla tov	good night
לישון	lishon	to sleep
לך	lecha	to you (m/s)
לך	lach	to you (f/s)
לכמה זמן?	lechama zman?	for how long
ללא עישון	lelo eishun	no smoking
ללכת	lalechet	to go
ללמוד	llmod	to learn
למחזר	lemachzer	to recycle
לנהוג	linhog	to drive
לנסוע	linsoa	to go by car
לעבוד	la'avod	to work
לעזור	la'azor	to help
לפנות	lifnot	to turn
לקום	lakum	to get up
לקנות	liknot	to buy
לקרוא	likro	to read
לראות	lir'ot	to see
לרוץ	larutz	to run
לשחות	lischot	to swim
לשחק	lesachek	to play
לשכור	liskor	to hire
לשלוח	lishloach	to send
לשמוע	lishmo'a	to hear
לשמור	lishmor	to keep, to guard
מ...	mey (like mail)	from
מאה	me'a	hundred
מאוד	meod	very
מאוחר	meuchar	late
מאי	My	May
מאתיים	matayim	two hundred

מבין	mevin	understand (m/s)
מבקש	mevakesh	ask for (m/s)
מגיע	magia	arrive (m/s)
מדבר	medaber	speak (m/s)
?מה שלומך	Ma shlomcha?	How are you? (m/s)
?מה שלומך	Ma shlomech?	How are you? (f/s)
מהר	maher	quickly
מודיעין	modieen	information
מוזמן	muzman	invited
מול	mul	opposite
מוסיקה	musika	music
מוסלמים	Muslemim	Moslems
מוקדם	mukdam	early
מזגן	mazgan	air conditioner
מזל טוב	Mazal tov	Congratulations
מחיר	mechir	price
מטבח	mitbach	kitchen
מטוס	matos	airplane
מי	mee	who
מידה	mida	size
מידי	miday	too much, too many
מיחזור	michzur	recycling
מייל	mail	mail
מיליון	million	million
מים	mayim	water
מכונית	mechonit	car
מכנסיים	michnasayim	trousers
מלוח	maluach	salty
מלון	malon	hotel
מלח	melach	salt
מלצר	meltzar	waiter
מלצרית	meltzarit	waitress
ממהר	memaher	hurry (m/s)

מנצח	menatzeach	winner (m/s) conductor
מסגד	Misgad	Mosque
מספיק	maspik	enough
מספר	mispar	number
מעדיף	ma'adif	prefer
מעט	me'at	a little, some
מעניין	me'anyen	interesting
מפה	mapa	map, table cloth
מצדה	Metzada	Masada
מצטער	mitzta'er	sorry (m/s)
מקלחת	miklachat	shower
מר	Mar	Mr
מרץ	Mertz	March
מרק	marak	soup
מרת	Marat	Mrs
משפחה	mishpacha	family
מתאים	mat'im	fit (m/s)
מתוק	matok	sweet
מתחיל	matchil	begin (m/s)
מתי?	Matay?	When?
מתנצל	mitnatzel	apologize (m/s)

נהג	nehag	driver
נובמבר	November	November
נוסע מ...ל...	nose'a me/le...	go by car (m/s) from/to...
נוצרים	Notzrim	Christians
נסיעה טובה	nesi'ah tova	bon voyage
נעים מאוד	naeem me'od	pleased to meet you
נצרת	Nazareth	Nazareth
נרות	nerot	candles

סבא	saba	grandfather
סבתא	savta	grandmother
סגור	sagur	closed

סודה	soda	soda
סוכות	Sukot	Feast of Tabernacles
סוכר	sukar	sugar
סוף	sof	end
סוף שבוע	sof shavua	weekend
סטודנט	student	student
סטייק	steak	steak
סכו״ם	sakum	cutlery
סלט	salat	salad
סליחה	slicha	sorry (apology)
ספגטי	spaghetti	spaghetti
ספורט	sport	sport
ספטמבר	September	September
ספל	sefel	cup
סרט	seret	film
עבודה	avoda	work
עברית	Ivrit	Hebrew
עד	ad	until
עובד	oved	work (m/s)
עוגה	uga	cake
עוד	od	more
עולה	ole	cost (m/s)
עם	eim	with
ערב	erev	evening
ערב טוב	erev tov	good evening
ערבית	Aravit	Arabic
עשר	eser	ten (f)
עשרה	asara	ten (m)
עשרים	esrim	twenty
פארק	park	park
פברואר	Februar	February

פופקורן	popcorn	popcorn
פורים	Purim	Purim (festival)
פחות	pachot	less
פינה	pina	corner
פיצה	pizza	pizza
פנסיונר	pensioner	pensioner
פסח	Pesach	Passover (festival)
פעם	pa'am	once
פעם בשבוע	pa'am beshavua	once a week
פתוח	patuach	open
צהוב	tzahov	yellow
צום	tzom	fast (abstain from eating)
צ'יפס	chips	chips
צלחת	tzalachat	plate
צריך ל...	tzarich le...	have to...
קולנוע	kolnoa	cinema
קומדיה	komedia	comedy
קונה	kone	buy (m/s)
קונצרט	kontzert	concert
קופה	kupa	box office
קטן	katan	small
קלאסי	klasy	classic
קם	kam	get up (m/s)
קפה	kafe	coffee
קצר	katzar	short
ראש השנה	Rosh hashana	Head of the year (Jewish New Year)
(יום) ראשון	(yom) rishon	first, Sunday
(יום) רביעי	(yom) reviee	fourth, (Wednesday)
רבע	reva	quarter

רדיו	radio	radio
רואה	r'oeh	see (m/s)
רופא	rofe	doctor
רוצה	rotze	want (m/s)
רוצה ל...	rotze le...	want to
רזה	raze	slim
רחוב	rechov	street
ריצה	ritza	running
ריקוד	rikud	dance
רישיון נהיגה	rishyon nehiga	driving licence
רכבת	rakevet	train
רמזור	ramzor	traffic light
רע	raa	bad
רציף	ratzif	platform
רק	rak	only, just
שבוע	shavua	week
שבועות	shvuot	weeks
שבועות	shavuot	First fruit festival
שביעי	shviee	seventh
שבע	sheva	seven (f)
שבע מאות	shva meot	seven hundreds
שבע עשרה	shva esre	seventeen (f)
שבעה	shiv'ah	seven (m)
שבעה עשר	shiv'ah asar	seventeen (m)
שבעים	shiv'iem	seventy
שבת	Shabbat	Saturday
שבת שלום	Shabbat shalom	Good Sabbath
שדה תעופה	sde teufa	airport
שולח	sholeach	send (m)
שולחן	shulchan	table
שופט	shofet	referee, judge
שוקולד	shokolad	chocolate

שותה	shote	drink (v. m/s)
שחור	shachor	black
שחייה	schiya	swimming
שחיין	sachyan	swimmer
שחקן	sachkan	actor
שיר	shir	song
שירותים	sheyrutim	lavatory
שירים	shirim	songs (p)
שישה	shisha	six (m)
שישה עשר	shisha asar	sixteen m
שישי	(yom) shishi	sixth, Friday
שישים	shishim	sixty
של	shel	of, belong to
שלום	shalom	hello, peace
שלוש	shalosh	three (f)
שלוש מאות	shlosh meot	three hundred
שלושה	shlosha	three (m)
שלושים	shloshim	thirty
שלישי	(yom) Shlishi	third, Tuesday
שם	sham	there
שם	shem	name
שמאל	smol	left
שמאלה	smola	to the left
שמונה	shmona	eight (m)
שמונה	shmone	eight (f)
שמונה עשר	shmona asar	eighteen (m)
שמונה עשרה	shmone esre	eighteen (f)
שמונים	shmonim	eighty
שמח	same'ach	happy
שמלה	simla	dress
שני	(yom) sheni	second, Monday
שניים	shnayim	two (m)

שעה	sha'a	hour
שש	shesh	six (f)
שש מאות	shesh meot	six hundred
שש עשרה	shesh esre	sixteen (f)
שתייה	ss	drink (n)
שתיים	shtayim	two (f)
תאריך	tt	date
תה	te	tea
תודה	todah	thanks
תזמורת	tizmoret	orchestra
תחנה	tachana	station
תיאטרון	tei'atron	theatre
תל-אביב	Tel-Aviv	Tel-Aviv
תלמיד	talmid	student
תמונה	tmuna	picture
תפריט	tafrit	menu
תשע	tesha	nine (f)
תשע עשרה	tsha esre	nineteen (f)
תשעה	tish'a	nine (m)
תשעה באב	Tish'a beav	Ninth of Ab (day of fasting)
תשעה עשר	tish'ah asar	nineteen (m)
תשעים	tisheim	ninety

English–Hebrew glossary

Conventions

adj adjective; f feminine; m masculine; n noun; v verb; p plural; s singular

a little, some	מעט	me'at
actor	שחקן	sachkan
Africa	אפריקה	Africa
airplane	מטוס	matos
airport	שדה תעופה	sde-teufa
America	אמריקה	America
and	ו...	ve
apologize (m/s)	מתנצל	mitnatzel
April	אפריל	April
Arabic	ערבית	Aravit
arrive (m/s)	מגיע	magi'a
Asia	אסיה	Asia
ask for (m/s)	מבקש	mevakesh
August	אוגוסט	August
Australia	אוסטרליה	Ostralia
bad	רע	ra
ballerina	בלרינה	ballerina
ballet	בלט	ballet
bank	בנק	bank
bar	בר	bar
bar mitzvah	בר-מצווה	bar-mitzvah
basketball	כדורסל	kadursal
bath	אמבטיה	ambatia
beautiful	יפה	yafe

because	כי	kee
bedroom	חדר שינה	chadar sheyna
begin (m/s)	מתחיל	matchil
Bethlehem	בית-לחם	Beit-lechem
big (adj m)	גדול	gadol
birthday party	חגיגת יום-הולדת	chaigat yom huledet
black	שחור	shachor
blue	כחול	kachol
bon appétit	בתאבון	beteavon
bon voyage	נסיעה טובה	nesi'a tova
box office	קופה	kupa
breakfast	ארוחת בוקר	aruchat boker
brother	אח	ach
bus	אוטובוס	otobus
buy (m/s)	קונה	kone
cake	עוגה	uga
can (m/s)	יכול	yachol
candles	נרות	nerot
can't (m/s)	לא יכול	lo yachol
car	מכונית	mechonit
cheap	זול	zol
cheers	לחיים	lechayim
chips	צ'יפס	chips
chocolate	שוקולד	shokolad
Christians	נוצרים	Notzrim
Church	כנסייה	Knesia
cinema	קולנוע	kolnoa
classic	קלאסי	classi
cloth	בגד	bèged
clothes	בגדים	b'gadim
coffee	קפה	kafe
come (m/s)	בא	ba

comedy	קומדיה	komedia
concert	קונצרט	kontzert
congratulations	מזל טוב	mazal tov
corner	פינה	pina
cost m/s	עולה	Ole
country	ארץ	eretz
couple	זוג	zug
cup	ספל	sefel
cutlery	סכו"ם	sakum
dance (v)	ריקוד	rikud
dark	כהה	kehe
date	תאריך	ta'arich
daughter, girl	בת	bat
day	יום	yom
December	דצמבר	Detzember
diet	דיאטה	dieta
dining room	חדר אוכל	chadar ochel
dinner, supper	ארוחת ערב	aruchat erev
doctor	רופא	rofe
dollar	דולר	dollar
don't love (m/s)	לא אוהב	lo o'hev
double room	חדר זוגי	cheder zugi
dress	שמלה	simla
drink (n)	שתייה	shtiya
drink (v. m/s)	שותה	shote
driver	נהג	nehag
driving licence	רישיון נהיגה	rishyon nehiga
early	מוקדם	mukdam
eat (v s/m)	אוכל	ochel
eight f	שמונה	shmone
eight m	שמונה	shmona
eighteen f	שמונה עשרה	shmone esre

eighteen m	שמונה עשר	shmona asar
eighty	שמונים	shmonim
Eilat (town)	אילת	Eilat
eleven f	אחת עשרה	achat esre
eleven m	אחד עשר	achad asar
end	סוף	sof
English	אנגלית	Anglit
enough	די	day (like die)
Europe	אירופה	Eiropa
evening	ערב	erev
every day	כל יום	kol yom
every hour	כל שעה	kol sha'a
expensive	יקר	yakar
family	משפחה	mishpacha
farmer	איכר	Ikar
fast (abstain from eating)	צום	tzom
father	אבא	aba
February	פברואר	Februar
festival	חג	chag
fifteen (f)	חמש עשרה	chamesh esre
fifteen (m)	חמישה עשר	chamish asar
fifth (Thursday)	יום חמישי	yom chamishi
fifty	חמישים	chamishim
film	סרט	seret
First fruit festival	שבועות	Shavuot
first, Sunday	יום ראשון	(yom) rishon
fit (m/s)	מתאים	mat'im
fitness	כושר	Kosher
five (f)	חמש	chamesh
five hundred	חמש מאות	chamesh me'ot
five (m)	חמישה	chamisha
food	אוכל	ochel

football	כדורגל	kaduregel
For how long?	כמה זמן?	Kama zman?
forty	ארבעים	arba'im
four (f)	ארבע	arba
four (m)	ארבעה	arba'a
fourteen (f)	ארבע עשרה	arba esre
fourteen (m)	ארבעה עשר	arba'a asar
fourth, (Wednesday)	רביעי	(yom) Reviee
friend	חבר	chaver
from	מ...	me...

get up m/s	קם	kam
giraffe	ג'ירף	giraffe
glass (drinking)	כוס	kos
go by car m/s from ... to ...	נוסע מ ... ל ...	nos'a me ...le ...
go (m/s)	הולך	holech
goes out m/s	יוצא	yotze
good	טוב	tov
good evening	ערב טוב	erev tov
good morning	בוקר טוב	boker tov
good night	לילה טוב	layla tov
good Sabbath	שבת שלום	shabat shalom
grandfather	סבא	saba
grandmother	סבתא	savta
green	ירוק	yarok
guest room	חדר אורחים	chadar orchim
guitar	גיטרה	gitara
gym	חדר כושר	chadar kosher

half	חצי	chatzi
hello, peace	שלום	shalom
Hanukah	חנוכה	Chanuka
Hanukah candelabra	חנוכיה	Chanukia

happy	שמח	sameach
happy holiday	חג שמח	chag same'ach
have to	צריך	tzarich
he	הוא	hoo
Head of the year (Jewish New Year)	ראש השנה	Rosh hashana
Hebrew	עברית	Ivrit
helicopter	הליקופטר	helicopter
here is the...	הנה ה...	hine ha...
high-tech	היי-טק	high-tec
hit	להיט	hahit
home, house	בית	bayit
hotel	מלון	malon
hour	שעה	sha'a
How are you? (f/s)	מה שלומך	Ma shlomech?
How are you? (m/s)	מה שלומך	Ma shlomcha?
How long?	כמה זמן	Kama zman?
How much does it cost?	כמה זה עולה	Kama ze ole?
How much, how many?	כמה	Kama?
hundred	מאה	me'a
hurry (m/s)	ממהר	memaher
I	אני	ani
I have	יש לי	yesh li
in	ב	be
information	מודיעין	mm
interesting	מעניין	meanyen
internet	אינטרנט	internet
invitation	הזמנה	hazmana
invited	מוזמן	muzman
Israel	ישראל	Yisrael
Jaffa	יפו	Yafo
January	ינואר	Yanuar

jazz	ג'אז	jazz
jeep	ג'יפ	jeep
Jerusalem	ירושלים	Yerushalayim
Jews	יהודים	Yehudim
judo	ג'ודו	judo
July	יולי	Yuli
June	יוני	Yuni
kitchen	מטבח	mitbach
late	מאוחר	me'uchar
lavatory	שרותים	sherutim
left	שמאל	smol
less	פחות	pachot
live, dwell (v.m)	גר	gar
long	ארוך	aroch
love (m/s)	אוהב	ohev
lunch	ארוחת צהריים	aruchat tzohorayim
mail	מייל	mail
map, table cloth	מפה	mapa
March	מרץ	Mertz
Masada	מצדה	Metzada
May	מאי	May
May I help?	?אפשר לעזור	Efshar la'azor?
meal	ארוחה	arucha
menu	תפריט	tafrit
milk	חלב	chalav
million	מיליון	million
minute	דקה	daka
money	כסף	kesef
month	חודש	chodesh
more	יותר	yoter
morning	בוקר	boker

Moslems	מוסלמים	Muslemim
Mosque	מסגד	Misgad
mother	אמא	ima
Mr	מר	Mar
Mrs	מרת	Marat
much, many	הרבה	harbe
music	מוסיקה	musika

name	שם	shem
Nazareth	נצרת	Natzeret
near the...	ליד	leyad ha...
new (m)	חדש	chadash
night	לילה	layla
nine (f)	תשע	tesha
nine (m)	תשעה	tish'a
nineteen (f)	תשע עשרה	tsha esre
nineteen (m)	תשעה עשר	tish'a asar
ninety	תשעים	tish'im
ninth of Ab day of fasting	תשעה באב	Tish'a be'av
no	לא	lo
no smoking	לא לעשן	lo leashen
November	נובמבר	November
number	מספר	mispar

October	אוקטובר	October
of, belong to	של	shel
once	פעם	pa'am
once a week	פעם בשבוע	pa'am beshavua
one (f)	אחת	achat
one (m)	אחד	achad
only, just	רק	rak
open	פתוח	patuach
opera	אופרה	opera

opposite	מול	mul
orange	כתום	katom
orchestra	תזמורת	tizmoret
park	פארק	park
party	חגיגה	chagiga
Passover	פסח	Pesach
pensioner	פנסיונר	pensioner
picture	תמונה	tmuna
pink	ורוד	varod
pizza	פיצה	pizza
plate	צלחת	tzalachat
platform	רציף	ratzif
please	בבקשה	bevakasha
Pleased to meet you	נעים מאוד	Na'im meod
popcorn	פופקורן	Pp
possible	אפשר	efshar
post	דואר	doar
prefer (m)	מעדיף	ma'adif
price	מחיר	mechir
Purim (festival)	פורים	Purim
quarter	רבע	reva
quickly	מהר	maher
radio	רדיו	radio
recycling	מיחזור	michzur
red	אדום	adom
referee, judge	שופט	shofet
request	בקשה	bakasha
return (ticket)	הלוך ושוב	haloch vashov
right	ימין	yamin
room	חדר	cheder
running (v)	ריצה	ritza

sugar	סוכר	sukar
salad	סלט	Salat
salt	מלח	melach
salty	מלוח	maluach
Saturday	שבת	Shabbat
school	בית ספר	beit-sefer
Second, Monday	שני	Yom Sheni
see (m/s)	רואה	ro'e
see you	להתראות	Lehitra'ot
send (m)	שולח	sholeah
September	ספטמבר	September
seven (f)	שבע	sheva
Ss	שבע מאות	shva meot
seven m	שבעה	shiv'a
Ss	שבע עשרה	Ss
seventeen (m)	שבעה עשר	shiv'a asar
seventh	שביעי	shvi'ee
seventy	שבעים	shiv'im
she	היא	hee
shirt	שיר	chultza
shop	חנות	chanut
short	קצר	katzar
show	הצגה	hatzaga
shower	מקלחת	miklachat
sister, nurse	אחות	Achot
six (f)	שש	shesh
six hundred	שש מאות	shesh me'ot
six (m)	שישה	Ss
sixteen (f)	שש עשרה	shesh esre
sixteen (m)	שישה עשר	shisha asar
sixth , Friday	שישי	(yom) Shishi
sixty	שישים	shishim
size	מידה	mida

slim (m)	רזה	ra'ze
slowly	לאט	le'at
small	קטן	katan
soda	סודה	soda
son, boy	בן	ben
song	שיר	shir
songs	שירים	shirim
sorry (apology)	סליחה	slicha
sorry (m/s)	מצטער	Mitztaer
soup	מרק	marak
spaghetti	ספגטי	spaghetti
speak (m/s)	מדבר	medaber
sport	ספורט	sport
stage	במה	bama
station	תחנה	tachana
steak	סטייק	steak
street	רחוב	rechov
student	סטודנט	student
study (m/s)	לומד	lomed
sugar	סוכר	sukar
suit	חליפה	chalifa
sweet	מתוק	matok
swimmer	שחיין	sachyan
swimming	שחייה	schiya
synagogue	בית כנסת	beit kneset
Tabernacles Feast of	סוכות	Sukkot
table	שולחן	shulchan
tall, high m	גבוה	gavo'ha
tasty	טעים	taim
taxi	טקסי	Tt
tea	תה	te
Tel-Aviv	תל-אביב	Tel-Aviv

150

telephone	טלפון	telephone
television	טלביזיה	televizia
ten (f)	עשר	eser
ten (m)	עשרה	asara
tennis	טניס	tennis
thanks	תודה	toda
the	ה	ha
the next, the coming m/s	הבא	ha'ba
theatre	תיאטרון	teatron
there	שם	sham
there is...	יש	yesh
there is no...	אין	ein
they (f)	הן	hen
they (m)	הם	hem
third, Tuesday	שלישי	(yom) Shlishi
thirty	שלושים	shloshim
this, that (f/s)	זאת	zot
this, that (m/s)	זה	ze
three f	שלוש	shalosh
three hundred	שלוש מאות	shlosh me'ot
three m	שלושה	shlosha
ticket	כרטיס	kartis
time	זמן	zman
timetable	לוח זמנים	luach-zmanim
tip	טיפ	tip
to ask for	לבקש	levakesh
to be	להיות	liheyot
to be late	לאחר	leacher
to begin	להתחיל	lehatchil
to buy	לקנות	liknot
to change	להחליף	lehachalif
to drive	לנהוג	linhog
to eat	לאכול	le'echol

to fly	לטוס	latus
to get up	לקום	lakum
to go	ללכת	lalechet
to go by car	לנסוע	linso'a
to go on a trip	לטייל	letayel
to hear	לשמוע	lishmo'a
to help	לעזור	la'azor
to hire	לשכור	liskor
to keep, to guard	לשמור	lishmor
to learn	ללמוד	lilmod
to me	לי	li
to order	להזמין	lehazmin
to play	לשחק	lesachek
to read	לקרוא	likro
to recycle	למחזר	lemachzer
to run	לרוץ	larutz
to see	לראות	llr'ot
to send	לשלוח	lishlo'ach
to sleep	לישון	lishon
to surf	לגלוש	liglosh
to swim	לשחות	lischot
to the left	שמאלה	smola
to the right	ימינה	yamina
to turn	לפנות	lifnot
to work	לעבוד	la'avod
to you (f/s)	לך	lach
to you (m)/s	לך	lecha
too much, too many	יותר מידי	yoter miday
too, as well	גם	gam
tractor	טרקטור	tractor
traffic light	רמזור	ramzor
tragedy	טרגדיה	tragedia
train	רכבת	rakevet
training	אימון	imun

trousers	מכנסיים	michnasayim
turquoise	טורקיז	turkiz
twenty	עשרים	esrim
two (f)	שתיים	shtayim
two (m)	שניים	shnayim
two hundred	מאתיים	maatayim
understand (m/s)	מבין	mevin
university	אוניברסיטה	universita
until	עד	aad
very	מאוד	me'od
waiter	מלצר	meltzar
waitress	מלצרית	meltzarit
want m/s	רוצה	rotze
want to	...רוצה ל	rotze le...
water	מים	Mm
we	אנחנו	anachnu
wedding	חתונה	chatuna
week	שבוע	shavua
weekend	סוף השבוע	sof shavua
weeks	שבועות	shavu'ot
What, which? (f)	?איזו	Eizo?
What, which (m)	?איזה	Eize?
When?	?מתי	Matay?
Where?	?איפה	Eifo?
Where to?	?לאן	Le'an?
white	לבן	lavan
Who?	?מי	Mi?
winner (m/s) conductor	מנצח	menatzeach
wine	יין	yayin
with	עם	Im
work (n)	עבודה	avoda
work (v m/s)	עובד	oved

working day	יום עבודה	yom avoda
yellow	צהוב	tzahov
you (f/p)	אתן	aten
you (f/s)	את	at
you (m/p)	אתם	atem
you (m/s)	אתה	ata
zebra	זברה	zebra